THE VISIONARY H

Nevill Drury was born in England in 1947 but has lived most of his life in Australia. An internationally published author in the fields of holistic health and the esoteric traditions, he has a long-standing interest in research into different states of consciousness. Among his special interests are shamanism and visionary art.

He holds a Master's degree in anthropology and is a former editor of *Nature & Health* journal.

BY THE SAME AUTHOR

Don Juan, Mescalito and Modern Magic
The Elements of Human Potential
The Elements of Shamanism
Healing Music
The Healing Power
Inner Health (ed)
Inner Visions
Music for Inner Space
The Shaman and the Magician
Vision Quest

The Visionary Human

MYSTICAL CONSCIOUSNESS
AND
PARANORMAL PERSPECTIVES

NEVILL DRURY

E L E M E N T

Shaftesbury, Dorset • Rockport, Massachusetts

Published in Great Britain in 1991 by
Element Books Limited
Longmead, Shaftesbury, Dorset

Published in the USA in 1991 by
Element Inc
42 Broadway, Rockport, MA 01966

Cover design by Max Fairbrother
Designed by Roger Lightfoot
Typeset by Burns and Smith Ltd
Printed and bound in Great Britain by
Billings Ltd, Hylton Road, Worcester

British Library Cataloguing in Publication Data

Drury, Nevill, *1947–*
The visionary human: mystical consciousness and
paranormal perspectives.
I. Title
133.092

ISBN 1-85230-206-2

Contents

For Quentin

Acknowledgements

In recent years I have been privileged to meet a number of fellow-travellers concerned with exploring the potentials of human consciousness. They have, of course, profoundly influenced my perspectives, and some of them are referred to in this book.

My thanks to Charles Tart, Michael Harner, Kenneth Ring, Terence McKenna, John Lilly, Stanislav Grof, Timothy Leary and especially to Robert Monroe – who graciously agreed to the interview which appears here as Appendix 1.

‘Beyond words, in the silencing of thought, we are already there’

Alan Watts

‘All matter and energy in the universe is just frozen information.

Dr Timothy Leary

1.

Beyond Appearances

The word 'visionary' means different things to different people. For some it has the connotation of one who is a dreamer, who is out of touch with reality, or who spends time speculating on essentially impractical ideas or schemes. However a visionary may also be a person who sees more clearly, who can anticipate possibilities and who can look beyond appearances. This is the emphasis I am adopting here, for I am concerned primarily with the visionary as a person who has *greater* access to states of reality than is normally the case. Note that I used the word 'states' in the plural: much of this book will deal with the concept that there are many planes of reality available to human perception and that our normal consciousness restricts us to but a small range within the spectrum of experiential possibilities.

An interesting example of what I am referring to here is provided by an artist I know who suffered both a near-death experience and a stroke that left him partially paralysed. However, as a result of these experiences he had a highly developed 'psychic' awareness: he was able to project his consciousness beyond his body, see through physical walls and observe discarnate human forms in the street outside his house. These forms would come and go and seemed to co-exist quite happily with physical reality. This particular artist is quite a down-to-earth person and had no belief in 'ghosts' prior to his stroke. However, he became curious about who these spectral beings were. When he described their appearances to his neighbours he discovered that he was actually able to identify some of them as deceased former residents of the street where he lived.

Examples of this sort are a challenge to our familiar concepts of 'reality'. I am taking the position here – unashamedly, but supported, I believe, by a large body of evidence – that mystics, artists and visionaries who explore transpersonal and paranormal realms of consciousness have access to a broader terrain of sensory and inspirational information.

There is no doubting that the area of mysticism, visionary consciousness and the paranormal will, to some, seem very suspect indeed. However, I hope that even sceptics will find some encouragement here at least to raise questions about what we regard as 'normal reality'. After all, our scientifically developed world-view in modern western society is itself an intellectual construct and, while it has served us well, there are clear signs that our paradigms of reality are in need of some revision – or at least *expansion*. Such concepts as mystical enlightenment and visionary consciousness are, for most people, at the edge of normal human experience. Events of this sort do not happen very often and are certainly not mainstream in terms of the everyday reality most of us are familiar with. But then our particular society, which emphasizes a pragmatic materialist approach to reality, does not like to dwell overmuch on areas of human experience which are difficult to quantify, measure or anticipate. Our scientific method, which demands replication, insists that new hypotheses be tested against what has been systematically established already. This is all well and good, but it means that our world-view is necessarily and inherently reductionist. When new types of data come along that impinge on our dominant paradigms, our first instinct is to ignore them or sweep them under the carpet.

I believe that much of the emerging paranormal data falls into this 'too hard' category. As readers will see later in this book, there are profound implications for philosophy, science, psychology and religion in the now extensive evidence relating to out-of-the-body consciousness and the near-death experience. It also seems to me that we need to devote more particular attention to the study of altered states of consciousness in general, for such states are an intrinsic part of the human condition.

The eminent American psychologist Dr Charles Tart has proposed the idea of 'state-specific sciences' – sciences where the mode of investigation is specifically adapted to the area it is investigating. Tart has emphasized that it is rather difficult for a scientist used to exploring physical processes to be equally adept at evaluating such inner workings of the psyche as mystical consciousness or out-of-the-body perception – especially if he has had no personal experience of states like these.[1] And it is worth emphasizing that our modern western science, for all its achievements, has its greatest expertise in dealing with and exploring *external* reality. It is much less at home accounting for the events which arise in the inner world of the mind and spirit.

Nevertheless, as human beings, we all recognize that we live both in the outer and inner worlds of experience. Our brains and nervous systems receive stimuli from the external world and, through complex processes of sensory coding, establish an operative perceptual reality in which we can function. Understandably, most of us assume that 'reality is out there' but in fact the world we perceive is only a construction. The human brain is the end-product of some 3000 million years of biological evolution and the reason we see the way we do, and agree substantially on a 'consensus reality', is because as human beings we have all evolved with comparable faculties. The psychologist Dr Robert Ornstein expresses this very succinctly as follows:

> Personal consciousness is outward oriented [and] seems to have evolved for the primary purpose of ensuring individual biological survival...We first select the sensory modalities of personal consciousness from the mass of information reaching us. This is done by a multi-level process of filtration, for the most part sorting out survival-related stimuli. We are then able to construct a stable consciousness from the filtered input.[2]

So is the world of physical reality the only reality? The data on parapsychology, mysticism and visionary consciousness, as well as information provided by the study of cognitive anthropology, mythology and comparative religion, suggests it is not. It is through the inner world of the psyche – that fluid domain of inspirational images, dreams, fantasies and sacred archetypes – that human cultures have derived their mythologies, cosmologies, religious beliefs, art, music and literature. The psyche, after all, is the wellspring of creativity and it is through imagery that the inner realms are revealed to us.

As Mike and Nancy Samuels note in their exemplary book

Seeing With The Mind's Eye: 'An image held in the mind...is a direct experience of the inner world. In the outer world we are limited by the laws of matter in what we can experience. In the inner world there is no limit to what we can experience.'[3]

If this is so, why do so many members of our philosophical and scientific community play down its significance? Freud regarded mystical consciousness not as an experiential breakthrough but as a regression to a primitive, infantile state of human development. Professor Richard Gregory, a former Director of the Brain and Perception Laboratory at the University of Bristol, has been similarly disparaging:

> To the mystic, dreams and hallucinations are insights into another world of reality and truth. To these thinkers the brain is a hindrance to understanding – a filter between us and a supraphysical reality...To the more down-to-earth, however, including the empiricist philosophers...the brain is to be trusted only in health, and hallucinations, although interesting and perhaps suggestive, are no more than aberrant outputs of the brain, to be mistrusted and feared...To physiologists hallucinations and dreams are due to spontaneous activity of the brain, unchecked by sensory data.[4]

Dr Steven Rose, Professor of Biology at Britain's Open University, has similarly written in his book *The Conscious Brain*: 'It is highly probably that in due course it will be possible to explain the "mystic experience" in terms of neurobiology.' Like Professor Gregory, Rose's view of mystical and visionary experience is that essentially it is a pathological condition.

> The techniques of obtaining a mystic experience are all, whether quick and chemical or long and physical, those of diminishing the effectiveness of the cortex, of temporarily blasting some of its circuits, by means of food or sleep deprivation, or by excessive sensory input, or by thrusting a biochemical spanner into the cerebral works...In so far as the function of the brain is to enable the organism to exist in harmony with, survive in, operate upon, and understand the environment of its owner, the non-mystic brain manifestly functions better than the mystic one. The survival value of the mystic experience is low, and in evolutionary terms its

potential or desirability is clearly equally low. Like poetry, music and art, its effects may be a moving and significant part of the experience of being human. But so, for some, may be the artificial induction of an epileptic fit by stroboscopic flashes.[5]

However, such perspectives are really predicated on a conventional assumption of what it means to be 'normal'. Orthodox Western psychology and biology tend to regard human consciousness simply as a by-product of the electrochemical functioning of the brain and nervous system. Human beings consist at a fundamental level of a cluster of physical parts – a skeleton, muscles, tendons, a system of veins and arteries, internal organs, sense receptors and a nervous system – and when these parts function efficiently together, such humans are able to operate and perceive the *real* world. As Dr Gunther Stent, Professor of Molecular Biology at the University of California, Berkeley, has put it:

> Most biologists are...naïve realists, just as are most practising scientists. Like people-in-the-street, they believe that there exists a real world of things external to them and independent of their experience of it – and that this real world actually is as they see, hear, feel and smell it.[6]

So any departure from normal brain function is by definition abnormal, any venture into altered states of consciousness necessarily 'pathological'. After all, as Dr Gregory has noted, our normal perceptual filter processes restrict such psychic imagery from waking consciousness and thereby keep us 'sane'.

However, the situation may not be as clear-cut or as self-evident as these conventional perspectives suggest. One can pose the question: What if we were able to integrate such visionary impressions into our consciousness without having them disrupt our external reality? What if we could integrate these psychic events in such a way that they could enrich our lives rather than unleash a state of confusion or disorder? This, I would suggest, is the crux of the issue: it is not the visionary images themselves which are the problem; it is how we assimilate and apply such perceptions in our lives. A misguided teenager who takes LSD and then drives a car off a cliff-edge while under the illusion that he can fly like an eagle has clearly failed to integrate the visionary impressions he has received in his altered state. But an artist or musician whose creative vision enables him to communicate more sensitively, or with greater insight and expression, has certainly used his intuitive faculties to great benefit. So it is more a matter of how we engage ourselves in the visionary encounter with the mind than whether the information reaching our brains derives from a 'real' or an 'imaginary' source.

Nevertheless, such states are not always easy to describe and this is possibly a reason for their lack of scientific recognition. Mystics have often referred to transcendental experiences as 'awesome' or 'ineffable', but terms like these do little to convey the transformational qualities of such experiences.

Fortunately, while researching this book, I was able to discuss this issue with the well-known consciousness researcher, Dr Timothy Leary. His response was very much to the point:

> The brain processes 125 million signals per second, so there's a lot of show-biz going on inside the brain. In the psychedelic or visionary experience the brain operates using algorithms which are much more complex, but essentially similar to those used by a computer. All through history, mystics and visionaries have come back from their experiences saying 'Wow, it's ineffable – you can't put it into words.' Words are just lumbering along at two or three a second and your brain is pouring out at 125 million signals a second. Great artists occasionally have come back from their voyages within with 'still shots' or 'snap shots', as it were. Hieronymus Bosch is one who comes to mind. The great visionary musicians and film-makers all have the ability to make explicit some of the wonder and complexity of the inner panorama...All matter and energy in the universe is just frozen information.[7]

At this stage we should also distinguish between the words 'mystical' and 'visionary' since for many people they do not mean the same thing. The great Swiss psychologist, Carl Jung, believed that mysticism was a fundamental category of human experience and that it was grounded in the encounter between the ego and the 'numinous' – such psychospiritual events taking place deep in the collective unconscious, or the mythic levels of the mind. However, other commentators have distinguished between western mysticism, which places more emphasis on visions and revelations, and eastern mysticism, which regards visionary imagery as essentially illusory. As Dr Arthur Deikman explains, mysticism takes us finally beyond form and appearance: 'Repeatedly the mystical literature stresses that sensate experiences are not the goal of mysticism; rather it is only when these are transcended that one attains the aim of a *direct* (intuitive) knowledge of fundamental reality.'[8]

Visionaries, on the other hand, are evoking images through their various approaches to the inner world: they can manifest them in their art, literature or religious belief systems. Some of these images may derive from relatively accessible regions of the psyche while more archetypal content comes from deeper and more profound levels. Some images, too, are metaphors pointing beyond form to the transcendent mystical reality Deikman is referring to.

So while visionary consciousness is a less transcendent realm of perception than the mystical experience of Unity Consciousness, any substantial expansion of our perceptual horizons beyond the purely physical is impressive enough. Even such transitional 'visionary' stages of consciousness demand new psychological refinements and revised frameworks of scientific evaluation. Out-of-the-body and near-death experiences are difficult to explain in terms of materialist reductionism and it would seem that, from a paranormal viewpoint, a return to some sort of variation on Descartes' mind/body dualism is called for. In operative waking consciousness, mind and body clearly function in tandem, but states of dissociative visionary consciousness require a very different model of causality. And while orthodox neurobiologists may be quite convinced that the physical brain is the source of consciousness, as the noted philosopher and psychologist William James observed, it is by no means obvious, in terms of scientific observation, whether consciousness is *generated by* the brain or *transmitted through* it. As we will see, the paranormal evidence suggests strongly that the latter is the case.

My own belief is that the projection of consciousness beyond the normal frame of reference lies at the very heart of visionary illumination. A visionary, in these terms, is one who can transcend his familiar environs and enter the inner world of imaginal reality. Sometimes this inner journey may head off on a kind of psychic meandering but at other times it undoubtedly leads to experiential breakthroughs and even towards the mystical attainment of Unity Consciousness itself.

The visionary process can be disarmingly simple, as the following description of inspirational Taoist artists indicates.

> Chinese painters are said to have lived for weeks on end in the mountains and forests, among animals, or even in the water, in order to lose themselves completely in nature. Mi Fei called an oddly shaped rock his brother; Fan K'uan (*circa* 1000 AD) lived in the mountains and forests, often spending the whole day upon a crag and gazing about him, just to drink the beauty of the countryside. Even when there was snow on the ground, he would wander to and fro by moonlight, staring determinedly ahead, to achieve inspiration. Kao K'o-ming (tenth century AD) loved darkness and silence; he used to roam about in the wild and spend days on end contemplating the beauty of peaks and woods, oblivious of himself. When he reached home again he retired to a room where he would not be disturbed and allowed his soul to pass beyond the bounds of this world. In this condition he produced his pictures.[9]

2.

Mystical Origins

All great historical religions have their origins in the visionary experience. Religions by their very nature are intended as pathways to a Greater Mystery, claiming to provide for their devotees a deeper and broader framework of spiritual understanding than that provided by our secular and materialistic models of reality.

Whether we think of this Greater Mystery as a god, a spirit or an energy, or regard it in an abstract way as the very basis of the manifested universe – a quantum dimension which provides the core life-force of our being – essentially we are dealing with a concept that transcends our intellectual understanding. This invariably leads us to employ the language of myth, symbol and metaphor as an expression of what lies beyond. Indeed, all religious and mystical systems make use of such metaphors to convey what they perceive to be a 'higher truth'.

With our limited perceptions as human beings – our spectrum of awareness limited by the complex filtering processes that maintain the consensus reality and thereby keep us 'sane' and 'rational' – we can never hope to grasp the total magnitude of the Greater Mystery. We may only hope to catch glimpses of infinity now and then – dipping our toes in, as it were, at the edge of the cosmic ocean. The sublime and awesome nature of this transcendent spiritual domain – the vast and infinite sea of mystical awareness – is what has inspired prophets and seers throughout the ages. Its radiant, numinous energy has flowed in turn into sacred art and music, given rise to profound and sensitive poetry, and provided the charismatic founders of religion with a vision of vast realms beyond. The personal experience of this mystical energy has also brought with it its own sense of certainty: the feeling that a greater depth of being has been revealed, that a more profound perspective on life has been attained, perhaps that 'God' has spoken…

We need to remember, though, that the encounter with the Greater Mystery is, by definition, an altered state of consciousness: a 'peak experience'. And yet the very nature of such a mystical state makes it difficult for those who have not experienced such profound levels of awareness first hand to understand what has occurred. In the case of institutionalized religions we often find the revelations of the founder-visionary perpetuated in specific ways by those with no personal perspective on the vastness of the original experience. In this way the sacred metaphors in visionary revelations may be reduced to literal assertions and dogma. Profound insights and perceptions which have arisen in the psyche of the visionary become 'miraculous events' on the physical plane and a cause, perhaps, of bitter doctrinal wrangling.

So often the damage and division associated with religious factions results from a fundamental misunderstanding of the core visionary experience itself – a literalism begins to assert itself which is then used by the religious followers to defend the 'unique' nature of the founder's revelation. In extreme instances the religious devotees may feel that God has revealed the teaching only to them and not to others; that the teaching is an exclusive revelation, never to be repeated, and even that followers of other teachings or doctrines will be damned for all eternity for failing to heed this unique revelation.

We can see in this type of thinking, quite obviously, vast possibilities for serious dissent. Such an approach implies that 'truth' can be exclusively captured, that one's own revelation of the Greater Mystery is the only one that can be considered 'authentic' or 'divine', that other revelations, occurring elsewhere on the planet, must necessarily be inferior, less enlightened, heretical and possibly even 'evil'.

In such ways, and in a variety of cultural settings, then, belief systems spawn and build, producing in turn self-perpetuating edifices of doctrine and dogma. Of course, as the edifice grows larger and becomes ever more rigid, this brings with it new types of conformity. The message to the followers from those in power may then become assertive: do not stray from these confines; here is the orthodox teaching – complete and unequivocal. Such an attitude provides us with the very basis for fanatical extremism and in some cases for religious wars. Fundamentalist Islam is a shining example in our own times.

Inevitably, problems like these arise some time after the initial visionary experiences have taken place and the religious founder has been elevated or 'mythologized' to a position of spiritual authority. And such problems, when they do arise, are usually brought on by the extremist views of the followers rather than by the visionary who received the revelations in the first instance. Almost without exception, conflict is caused by those with lesser vision – by those who feel an urge to protect their own specific cause, and who feel potentially threatened by those making competing claims elsewhere.

Founder Visionaries

At this point, then, it might be useful to consider the spiritual careers and visionary breakthroughs of three historical founders of religions, all of whom, in varying degrees, have had their core revelations institutionalized and their teachings variously interpreted by dissenting groups and factions. But by looking at the experiences of the founder-visionaries themselves we get an insight into the process of mystical revelation itself. Who better than to provide us with examples of spiritual transformation than the Buddha, Jesus and Muhammad?

Siddhartha Gautama Buddha (563 BC–483 BC)

The term 'Buddha', meaning 'enlightened one' was a name later given to the Indian prince Siddhartha Gautama, who was born in Lumbini Garden in the Himalayan foothills.

The accounts of Gautama's birth are unavoidably shrouded in mythic language. It is said that many aeons before, an ascetic called Sumedha had taken the vows of a Bodhisattva (a Buddha-to-be) and while in the Tushita Heaven determined that he would be reborn into the Shakya clan. His parents would be King Shuddhodhana, a ruler of this clan, and his wife Mayadevi.

According to legend, Mayadevi received Gautama into her

body in the form of a white elephant – a symbol of perfect wisdom and royal power – and when he was born, the trees in Lumbini Garden burst into beautiful blooms. Later a horoscope was drawn up which identified Gautama as a 'universal monarch' and an *arhat* – 'one worthy to be honoured'.

Gautama grew up in an environment of great privilege and luxury. Cared for by thirty-two nurses and provided with three palaces – each intended for different seasons of the year – he enjoyed a world filled with dancing, singing, beautiful music and fragrant flowers. He married his cousin, Yashodhara, when he was sixteen, and she subsequently gave birth to their son, Rahula.

However, Gautama's life of elegant seclusion was destined not to last. He urged his father to allow him to see the world at large – not realizing that it contained evil and suffering. And so, with Channa his charioteer he rode through the streets of the city on what was a transformative journey. He saw a wrinkled, toothless old man whose body was so weak with age he was bent over, supporting himself with a stick; he saw a diseased man, stricken with fever and pain; he saw a corpse wrapped in cloth and being carried by family and friends to the funeral pyre, and finally he saw a monk, serenely begging with a bowl in his hand. Gautama now felt he had to find the means whereby one could maintain such inner calm and composure in the face of the evils of human existence – old age, sickness and death.

Gautama began his spiritual quest with what is now known as 'The Great Renunciation'. On the very night that his son was born, and with the help of his servants, Gautama secretly left his courtyard, rode off on his horse Kanthaka and journeyed till daybreak. He removed his princely garments, donned the clothes of a huntsman and cut off his hair with a sword. From now on he would not be a prince but a seeker of enlightenment.

In due course he studied under Alara Kalama, practised yoga and engaged in severe dietary abstentions for a period of six years. But the physical toll eventually became intolerable:

> Like dried canes now became my arms and legs, withered through this extremely scanty diet; like the foot of a camel became my buttock; like a string of beads became my spinal

> column with the vertebrae protruding. Just as the roof-beams of an old house sharply protrude, so protruded my ribs; just as in a deep well the little water-stars far beneath are scarcely seen, so now in my eye-balls the sunken pupils were hardly seen; just as a gourd freshly cut becomes empty and withered in the hot sun, so now became the skin of my head empty and withered...[1]

Gautama remained completely immobile during his ascetic austerities. He sought no shade from the sun, wind or rain. However it eventually became apparent to him that both his body and his mind were deteriorating and he decided to break his fast to build up his strength. And yet, in ceasing austerities he did not revert to a life of sensuality, but decided to follow a 'middle path', allowing himself to beg for a little food now and then as he wandered around.

One day, at a place called Gaya, he decided he would sit down under a bodhi tree and would not rise again until he had found enlightenment. It is recorded that Gautama, who was then thirty-five years of age, sat beneath the bodhi tree for forty-nine days before becoming a Buddha.

During the forty-nine days, according to legend, Gautama was severely taunted by Mara, the Tempter. Mara is said to have offered Gautama dominion 'over the four great continents and their 2000 attending isles' but he responded by saying: 'I have no wish for sovereignty. I am about to make the 10,000 worlds thunder with my becoming a Buddha.'

Mara assembled a huge army and when he attacked Gautama all the gods in the 10,000 worlds fled, leaving him alone. Mara now launched against him a whirlwind, a huge rainstorm, showers of rocks, weapons, hot ashes and mud – but to no avail. Mara then taunted him, saying that there was no one to bear witness for him. Gautama, sitting in a lotus position with his left hand resting palm up on his right leg, now reached down with his right hand to touch the ground, thereby 'calling the earth to witness'.

According to legend, the earth is said to have thundered: 'I bear you witness' with 100, 1000, 100,000 roars...Then Mara withdrew, frustrated in his attempts to lure Gautama from his task.

Meanwhile the moon rose and Gautama passed into a state of

deep meditation. He reviewed his previous incarnations, rose to higher levels of consciousness where he was able to understand the nature of his human self, and finally attained a state of pure enlightenment, or Buddhahood.

After attaining enlightenment in this way, it is said that the Buddha remained in his meditative position for a further forty-nine days, contemplating the truths that had been revealed to him. Mara approached him again, tempting him to enter Nirvana, but Gautama decided instead to continue his earthly existence and share his spiritual knowledge with others.

He now travelled to Sarnath, a few miles north of Benares, and was joined by five ascetics who had left his company earlier, when he had broken his pattern of austerities. At Deer Park he gave a sermon which contained the four noble truths and the eightfold path. These teachings, in essence, were as follows:

* Life is suffering (*dukkha*).
* The cause of this suffering is desire (*tanha*).
* Suffering can be eliminated when desire is extinguished.
* Desire can be eliminated by pursuing the eightfold path which comprises:

  Right understanding
  Right aspiration
  Right speech
  Right conduct
  Right vocation
  Right effort
  Right mindfulness
  Right concentration

From this time onwards, Gautama Buddha believed that his main task was to bring the teaching (*Dhamma*) to the world, and he did this for a further forty-five years, gaining many converts and also ordaining his son Rahula. At his death he is said to have gone through a number of mystical states, finally entering *Parinibbana*, or total bliss.

Jesus (circa *4* BC–AD *33*)

According to the biblical account of Matthew, Jesus was born in humble circumstances. Mary was betrothed to a carpenter named Joseph but before they came together she discovered she was pregnant. Joseph felt he should separate from Mary to avoid any embarrassment but he then had a dream in which an angel told him: 'Joseph, son of David, do not fear to take Mary your wife, for that which is conceived in her is of the Holy Spirit; she will bear a son, and you shall call his name Jesus, for he will save his people from their sins.'[2]

Mary and Joseph travelled to Bethlehem to comply with a decree from Caesar Augustus that there was to be a census, and all Jews were to return to their place of tribal origin. Joseph and Mary arrived in Bethlehem and it was clear that she was about to give birth to Jesus. No rooms were available in the inn, so the couple spent the night in a stable. It was here that Jesus was born.

As with Gautama, Jesus' birth was nevertheless the occasion for dramatic portents. It was said that a star in the East indicated that the King of the Jews had been born, and three wise men from the East fell down and worshipped the child, offering him gifts of gold, frankincense and myrrh.

We know nothing certain about the early years of Jesus' life. In all likelihood he would have had a *bar mitzvah* at the age of thirteen and would have studied the Hebrew scriptures, probably receiving instruction at the local synagogue.

The turning point in his spiritual career came, however, when at the age of thirty he went to the River Jordan to be baptized by John the Baptist. John was himself a somewhat eccentric figure – he preached repentance in the wilderness of Judaea and subsisted on a diet of locusts and wild honey. It is also possible that he may have been the Teacher of Righteousness referred to in the Dead Sea Scrolls.[3] Many came to him to confess their wrongdoings and to be baptized. John proclaimed that his baptisms were of water, symbolizing repentance, but warned that a more formidable figure was coming: 'He who is coming after me is mightier than I, whose sandals I am not worthy to carry; he will baptize you with the Holy Spirit and with fire.'

Soon after this, Jesus presented himself to John to be baptized. According to Mark's account, 'When he came up out of the water, immediately he saw the heavens opened and the Spirit descending upon him like a dove; and a voice came from heaven: "Thou art my beloved son; with thee I am well pleased''.'[4] Inspired by this divine illumination – the Bible says he was 'driven by the Spirit' – Jesus wandered in the wilderness of Judaea, fasting for forty days. It was here that he was tempted by Satan in a similar way to Gautama's encounter with Mara.

Satan confronted Jesus with three temptations. First he challenged him, in his newly revealed role as the Son of God, to change stones into loaves of bread. Jesus resisted this act of magic. Then Satan took Jesus to the parapet of the Temple in the holy city of Jerusalem and challenged him to throw himself down, arguing that if he were really the Son of God he would be protected by the angels. Jesus resisted this act of potential egoism by declaring: 'You shall not tempt the Lord your God.' Then in the final temptation, Satan went with Jesus to a high mountain and showed him the different kingdoms of the world. Satan offered to give him these domains if he would in turn worship him as Lord – again, a comparable temptation to that of Mara. Jesus once again denied Satan, affirming: 'You shall worship the Lord your God, and only Him shall you serve.'

Jesus subsequently began to teach the love of God and one's fellow man, calling for everyone to repent of their sins in the assurance that God would be merciful to the righteous. He also counselled his disciples to pray to God in the manner described in Matthew's gospel ('Our Father, who art in Heaven...'), and according to John's gospel believed that baptism was essential for spiritual salvation: 'Unless one is born of water and the Spirit, one cannot enter the Kingdom of God.'

It can be argued that it was the confusion between spiritual and physical realities that led to Jesus' death. In several biblical accounts Jesus speaks of his role in terms that would seem extraordinarily egotistical were one to interpret them other than as statements made from a mystical perspective: 'I am the living bread that came down from Heaven'; 'Whoever eats of this bread will live for ever'; 'I am the light of the world; whoever follows me will not walk in darkness but will have the light of life'; 'You are from below, I am from above; you are of this world; I am not of this world'; 'I am the way and the truth and the life; no one comes to the Father but by me.'

In fact, it was because statements of this sort were taken literally that Jesus was condemned for blasphemy, brought to trial and crucified by the Roman governor, Pilate. Jesus was affirming that he had a special relationship with God – that, in his being, the Spirit was made flesh. When Jesus was taken before 'all the chief priests and the elders and the scribes' he was asked:

> 'Are you the messiah, the son of the Blessed?' Jesus said: 'I am, and you will see the Son of Man sitting at the right hand of Power and coming with the clouds of Heaven.' And the high priest tore his coat and said: 'Why should we need further witnesses? You have heard this blasphemy. What is your decision?' And they all condemned him as deserving death.[5]

Jesus clearly regarded his relationship with God the Father as extremely personal – a characteristic which distinguishes his visionary experiences from Eastern accounts of mystical illumination. His last words on the cross are recorded in the Psalm 22: '*Eli, Eli, lama sabachthani?*': 'My God, my God, why have you forsaken me?'

Nevertheless, Jesus' messianic role – or at least that ascribed to him by his followers – is clearly presented in the biblical accounts. According to the Gospel of Mark, following Jesus' resurrection and his miraculous appearance to the Apostles, Jesus gave a very clear, almost stark, statement of his religious purpose: 'Go into all the world and preach the gospel to all creatures. Whoever believes and is baptized will be saved…'

Muhammad (circa *AD 570–AD 632)*

Muhammad was born in Mecca, the son of prominent members of the Quraysh clan. His father, Abdullah, died a few days before he was born and his mother, Aminah, when he was only six years old. He was looked after by his grandfather Abd al Muttalib until he was eight and then, after his grandfather's death, by a paternal uncle, Abu Talib, who was the leader of the clan.

Muhammad grew up as a caravan trader on the camel routes. He is believed to have travelled with Abu Talib to Syria and also encountered other religious groups, including Jews and Christians. By the age of twenty-five he had been placed in charge of transporting the merchandise of a wealthy widow named Khadijah. She was fifteen years older than him and finally proposed that they be married. Muhammad accepted the offer and by all accounts their marriage was very happy. They had six children, the best known being Fatimah, and Muhammad took no other wives until Khadijah died in AD 619 (he is believed to have had eleven other wives later).

Khadijah's considerable wealth allowed Muhammad a certain amount of freedom and independence, and he liked to stay in the hills near Mecca. Sometimes he would visit a cave on Mount Hira, where he would engage in fasting, meditation and contemplation. It was during an all-night vigil towards the end of the month of Ramadan when he was forty years old that he experienced the first of several revelations – a vision of a majestic creature later identified as the archangel Gabriel. Gabriel demanded that Muhammad:

> Recite: 'In the Name of thy Lord who created,
> Created Man of a blood clot.'
> Recite: 'And thy Lord is the Most Generous,
> who taught by the Pen,'
> Taught Man that he knew not.'

The next morning, as he was leaving the cave he again heard the archangel's voice, this time proclaiming: 'Muhammad, you are Allah's messenger...' The archangel stood before him, bathed in brilliant light and Muhammad tried to turn his face away from the visionary being. However, at all turns Gabriel confronted him – then suddenly vanished. Muhammad now hurried home to tell Khadijah that either he was possessed by a spirit or truly called to the role of a prophet. Khadijah reassured him, believing that he had had an authentic revelation. She also told her Christian cousin, Warakah Ebn Nowfal, about Muhammad's experiences and he advised her that her husband had apparently encountered the same angel who had appeared to Moses. Muhammad had several further revelations, which he believed came directly from God, before his death in AD 632. During these experiences he would go into a cold sweat, and some commentators have suggested, probably incorrectly, that he may have suffered from epileptic fits. Be that as it may, Muhammad's revelations were sometimes written down and at other times memorized by his followers. Eventually they were collected and put into written form in AD 650. This collection of writings, the Quran (or Koran) – the sacred book of Islam – has remained unchanged to the present day.

Muhammad had grown up in a world abounding in idolatry. Mecca was dominated by the Sabian religion, whose devotees venerated the fixed stars and planets, and also a plurality of gods and spirits transposed into their culture from Graeco-Roman counterparts. The Temple of Mecca was consecrated to Zohal, or Saturn, and there were also Sabian counterparts of Jupiter, Mercury and Sirius the Dog Star. The Arabs around Mecca also worshipped a number of idols including the lion-shaped Yaghuth, and Hobal, introduced from Syria, who was believed to bring rain when required. Muhammad disliked idolatry instinctively, and after his revelations from Gabriel became determined to wipe it out altogether.

His principal cause as God's Prophet subsequently became to proclaim the worship of the One God – *Al Ilah*, or Allah. In due course Muhammad divided Islam (which means 'submission') into *Iman* (faith) and *Din* (practices, prayer, alms, fasting and the pilgrimage to Mecca). His teaching included belief in God, his angels, his scriptures, his prophets (Muhammad considered himself to be the last of twenty-eight prophets sent by God, his predecessors including Adam, Abraham, Jesus and John the Baptist), the resurrection and Day of Judgement, and God's control of good and evil.

Muhammad gained few converts at first – Khadijah was one, and so too were his cousin Ali, his adopted son Zyad, and a merchant named Abu-Bakr. Soon, however, the Quraysh clan into which he had been born came to regard Muhammad as a threat to their privileged position in Meccan society and he and his followers were persecuted and assaulted. At one point Muhammad's own life was in danger but his uncle Abu Talib was able to protect him. However, he urged Muhammad to abandon his new religious perspective.

When Abu Talib died in AD 619, Muhammad was once again vulnerable. However a delegation of twelve men who regarded themselves as Muslims, visited him from Medina (Yathrib) in AD 621, and the following year a larger group from this city invited him to join them. Muhammad agreed but, just before departing, he had to contend with an assassination plot. He was able to reach Medina, which lay some 200 miles north, in AD 622. His flight is now known as the *Hegira* or *Hijrah*, meaning 'to sever kinship ties'.

Subsequently, Muhammad helped to plan raids on caravans coming from Mecca and mounted a number of substantial military manoeuvres against the Meccan infantry and cavalry. In due course he negotiated treaties with the Meccans to remove the threat of raids from Medina and was able to procure the surrender of Mecca without bloodshed. Muhammad entered Mecca in AD 629, married the sister-in-law of his uncle, and after putting down a further Meccan uprising under Abu Sufyan, re-entered the city as both a political leader and the Prophet of God – a potent combination. At this time all remaining idols in the Ka'ba, the sacred centre of Mecca, were destroyed and Muhammad was able to proclaim the worship of Allah from both a spiritual and a political point of view.

The Transformation Experience

Obviously different social and political factors determine the continuation of a major religious faith, but when we consider the core transformative events in the lives of these three religious founders, distinct factors emerge, and these seem to be crucial components in the attainment of mystical experience.

All three had a clear sense of purpose, a desire to look beyond the more familiar domain of everyday existence and to open themselves to the universe on a broader level of understanding. Thus Gautama left the security of home and family to expand his horizons of experience. His resolve culminated, after many years, in forty-nine days of meditation spent beneath the bodhi tree in order to penetrate the mysteries of human existence iteslf. Jesus went to be with John the Baptist in the Judaean wilderness, and experienced the symbolic transformation of baptism, which became for him a rite of passage into the cosmos – the realm of spirit. And Muhammad sojourned in the hills near Mecca – a setting removed from domestic, trade and political issues, and the anathema of idolatry, where he could fast and meditate, attuning his mind to more spiritual concerns. It was in this setting – a remote cave on Mount Hira – and not amidst the clamour of the traders' caravans, that he received his revelations from Gabriel.

If we extrapolate these experiences in a contemporary way,

we might say that the Buddha, Jesus and Muhammad were each dispensing with their domestic 'programming' as a prelude to the core transformative experience. Both Buddha and Jesus had dramatic encounters with the Tempter – events which personify the universal battle with the forces of ego, vanity and pride, all manifestations of 'individual' rather than 'cosmic' consciousness.

All three, too, had withdrawn to an environmental setting that enabled them to focus on the inner, spiritual aspects of the universe rather than the external world, and each received his revelation while in an altered state of consciousness – states of awareness characterized in Gautama Buddha's case by profound philosophical insights into the nature of reality and, in the case of Jesus and Muhammad, by archetypal encounters with the Spirit (the voice and dove coming from God, and Gabriel serving as a 'messenger' from Allah).

To this extent then, the transformative experiences themselves appear not to have been accidental but occurred in the type of setting and context one would expect. The spiritual 'authority' of each of these religious leaders thus lies in the magnitude of the religious, spiritual and philosophical breakthroughs gained in each case. At the same time, we need to 'de-mystify' the process of mystical illumination in order to place it in an appropriate perspective. While the Buddha and Jesus have both been mythologized since their death (Gautama as a white elephant; Jesus born of a virgin), such metaphors are really an understandably human attempt to convey that the worlds of sacred and human reality have coexisted at special times in history. This need not be taken too literally, however. The real reason why humanity should revere Jesus, Muhammad and the Buddha is surely because they each had a special mystical capacity to perceive the world in a more profound and insightful way than most other human beings before or since. It is not so much that Jesus, for example, was the unique Son of God but that, for a unique moment, God, or Spirit, dwelt in him – that he was open to God and became 'one' with 'God the Father' in a privileged state of grace. Similarly, Buddha was able, during his meditations, to see beyond the veils of illusion to the domain of pure enlightenment, and Muhammad felt himself to be a messenger, or 'vehicle' for the oneness of Allah.

We see in such transformations a fusion of human and spiritual qualities on a profound level of awareness. Potentially, however, all human beings have the same capacity for such spiritual realization. The tragedy, if one can call it that, is that most of us live lives which filter such realizations from consciousness. If the Spirit lies all about as well as within us, if indeed we are all wanderers on the edge of the cosmic shore, then it is clearly of value to understand how the process of spiritual transformation might occur for each and every one of us. Indeed, one could hardly imagine a more worthwhile realm of inquiry.

I believe we can look at the factors relating to the visionary breakthrough quite dispassionately. Personally, I do not support the view that the Universal God-Energy has selected various individuals or groups in history and favoured them exclusively with divine revelations over other groups. Neither am I personally interested in ranking states of enlightenment or speculating whether the spiritual teachings of Jesus, for example, are 'superior' or 'inferior' to those of Muhammad or Gautama Buddha. Indeed, we are not obliged to look at the visionary process through the constraints of any particular belief system. Belief systems, as mentioned earlier, arise only after the visionary breakthrough has occurred. They gather momentum and build into doctrinal structures as the initial mystical impulse is transmuted by the prevailing cultural, political, linguistic, ethical and philosophical preferences of the particular society in which they occur. What we are considering here is the process which underlies and leads to the visionary experience in the first place – for if we can begin to understand that, it becomes potentially attainable for all of us.

It is not, then, a matter of following someone else's vision so much as discovering that infinite visionary source deep within oneself. However, this is not to say that one cannot learn profound lessons from those who have gone on ahead of us – simply that in the final analysis we owe it to ourselves to discover our own sacred depths. When we do this, our beliefs are enriched by our experience. If our realizations are sufficiently profound – tending towards states of transcendence and away from the ego – they will necessarily lead us towards feelings of connectedness with others and with the planet as a whole.

Interestingly, certain factors arise time and time again when we consider the visionary breakthrough as documented in the mystical literature. Here are some of the 'triggers' which can lead to altered states of consciousness. We usually find that some, though not necessarily all, are present in the mystical experience.

* Withdrawal from social 'programming'/sensory isolation
* Lifestyle modifications resulting in biochemical changes to the body (such as fasting and changes to the breathing cycle)
* A focus on inner attentiveness rather than the external world
* The use of symbols or ritual as a catalyst to attaining transcendental experiences
* A sense of personal openness and humility

Social Deprogramming/Sensory Isolation

If we accept the view that in everyday living we develop various routines and 'filters' for systematizing our daily activities, it follows that for any radically different mode of awareness to break through into consciousness a certain amount of 'deprogramming' – or at least a substantial shift in one's personal orientation – would have to occur first.

We find this phenomenon time and again in mystical and spiritual history. As noted earlier, Gautama Buddha, who had grown up in a privileged world of luxury and who had a particularly protected lifestyle, had his transformative vision only after leaving his protective context and encountering death, old age and suffering. Jesus had his profound spiritual insights at the River Jordan, while roaming the wilderness of Judaea or while reflecting silently in the Garden of Gethsemane. Muhammad withdrew from Mecca to the caves on Mount Hira, where he engaged in fasting, prayer and meditation.

However, revelatory or transformative mystical experiences are not confined to the founders of major religions. On a more familiar level we have a delightful account from one J. Trevor who describes in his autobiography, published in 1897, how a spiritual transformation occurred while he was walking with his dog in the countryside:

> One brilliant Sunday morning, my wife and boys went to the Unitarian Chapel in Macclesfield. I felt it impossible to

> accompany them – as though to leave the sunshine on the hills, and go down there to the chapel would be for the time an act of spiritual suicide. And I felt such need for new inspiration and expansion in my life. So, very reluctantly and sadly, I left my wife and boys to go down into the town, while I went further up into the hills with my stick and my dog. In the loveliness of the morning, and the beauty of the hills and valleys, I soon lost my sense of sadness and regret. For nearly an hour I walked along the road to the 'Cat and Fiddle', and then returned. On the way back, suddenly, without warning, I felt that I was in Heaven – an inward state of peace and joy and assurance indescribably intense, accompanied by a sense of being bathed in a warm glow of light, as though the external condition had brought about the internal effect – a feeling of having passed beyond the body, though the scene around me stood out more clearly and as if nearer to me than before, by reason of the illumination in the midst of which I seemed to be placed. This deep emotion lasted, though with decreasing strength, until I reached home, and for some time after, only gradually passing away.[6]

Trevor seems to have lost himself in the beauty of Nature, and his mood of 'sadness and regret' soon passed. When these personal emotional blockages had been removed he found that 'suddenly, without warning' he was in a state of heavenly bliss. Only after withdrawing from his familiar social setting and seeking greater inspiration in a more expansive and uplifting environment was he able to enter the right state of mind to attain the transformative vision.

In more recent times, too, many of us have become aware of the sensory isolation chambers, popularly known as 'float tanks' which are part of the holistic health scene. On an individual level these tanks do much the same thing as the cave did for Muhammad: they remove all awareness of the routine external world and allow the person floating in total darkness to focus within.

Developed by neurophysiologist Dr John Lilly, the tanks were designed on the basis that eliminating external stimuli would enhance the exploration of one's inner potential – especially with a view to developing one's creativity and intuition. The sensation of floating gravity-free in darkness and 'space' has led many adherents to experience feelings of inner security and a new sense of integration (see also Chapter Five).

Biochemical Changes in the Body

In the mystical traditions it has not been uncommon to engage in practices which alter the body's biochemistry. Some of these practices are primarily purificatory, while others may help facilitate altered states of consciousness.

Fasting is widely believed to act as a precursor to mystical revelations. Japanese Buddhists fast as part of their asceticism and as Dr Imamura Motoo has noted: 'Religious ascetics, who led their lives abstaining from food, came to the conclusion that fasting improved not only their spiritual state, but also their physical condition, and through fasting many diseases could be cured.'[7]

Fasting is a way of detoxifying the body and shedding excess body weight but it also helps practitioners to focus their spiritual resolve. Moses fasted for forty days and forty nights before receiving the Ten Commandments in a state of visionary consciousness on Mount Sinai, as did Elijah before reaching the Mount of God. Later Jesus continued this practice in the wilderness, and in the fourth century the forty-day period was officially adopted by the Christian Church as a time of preparation for Easter. Fasting was also practised in the Greek mystery cults as a prelude to receiving divine revelations in dreams.[8]

Techniques of breath control are similarly associated with altered states of consciousness and feature in both Indian *Pranayama* (breath yoga) and in modern holistic modalities like rebirthing and Holotropic Breath Therapy. The latter use a connected-breath cycle to produce a state of hyperventilation which can often appear rather dramatic, with spasms in the hands and feet. While hyperventilation is regarded in some medical circles as a pathological condition, Dr Stanislav Grof, the Czechoslovakian psychiatrist who developed Holotropic Breath Therapy, believes this type of breathing can be useful in overcoming emotional blockages.[9]

Physiologically, hyperventilation reduces the amount of oxygen transmitted to the cortex of the brain, producing a natural 'high'. It is therefore not surprising that techniques of hyperventilation and yogic breath retention have been used to attain mystical states of consciousness.

Inner Attentiveness

If we look beyond cultural differences, we find that all mystical traditions emphasize that we should pay less attention to our external self, or persona, and place more emphasis on our inner self, which is the pathway to our infinite and universal spiritual essence.

In modern western society most of us find that we are obliged to engage in activities which enhance our perception of distinctiveness. To attain success in the cut and thrust of contemporary life, we are obliged to project our personal image and to respond to external perceptions of who we are or should be. The focus is invariably on ego-fulfilment, on individual lives and careers, on pride in possessions – and with this, for many of us, comes a strong sense of competitiveness. We have to show that we are more efficient, more capable, more adept at business, more successful and assertive than others – these are the admired qualities in our culture. However, if this is the case, our lives are surely ego-dominated. By contrast, the mystical perspective urges us to look within, to pay attention instead to the realities beyond the world of ego – to touch the deep source of our inner nature which not only provides us with our core sense of *meaning* and *being* but also links us to all other living creatures and to the universe as a whole.

When we can add this depth of perception to our daily lives, our domestic and business activities take on an altogether different character. It is not, then, a case of competing against others but of working in tandem with them, of acknowledging different personal strengths and weaknesses while recognizing that all aspects of human endeavour are part of a broad spectrum of activity and fulfilment. It is from the broader viewpoint that we come to recognize a shared sense of purpose.

Fortunately, current political developments internationally give cause for renewed optimism. The leaders of the superpower countries seem now to be developing a more global perspective, a sense of international co-operation which rises above 'tribal' or nationalist power-play. On a domestic level we can apply the same sort of perspective. However we are more likely to do this if we practise some form of inner attentiveness, for that leads us towards our deeper, inner selves and towards a level of meaningful connectedness with others (see also Chapter Five).

Rituals and Symbols

As mentioned earlier, the visionary experience often comes about by withdrawing from the familiar external environment – which has its own patterning or automated behaviour patterns and expectations – to another domain where the inner self can be revealed. This can be an area of sensory isolation – a cave, a mountain-top or a desert – or, more close to home, in a float tank or in a private 'sacred space' at home that one has put aside as a meditation chamber. However, another approach has been used in the western magical traditions, and also in ritualistic temple settings within mainstream religion, and that is the use of sacred symbols to trigger transcendent awareness.

Using this approach, one comes to a sanctified place – a temple, a church, a special place in Nature. This domain is sacred: it is distinct from the outside or secular world. So churches are erected as 'houses of God' for religious ceremonies and occultists have private 'temples' where, within the ritual circle (itself a symbol of unity and wholeness), a sacred space is identified. This is a place dedicated to spiritual transformation. And in the same way that many Christian churches feature sacred images – representations of Jesus and the Virgin Mary and exquisite stained glass allowing the Spirit to break through into the everyday world – so, too, the ritual magician has on the walls of the temple motifs and symbols associated with the mystical task at hand. It may be that the magician wishes to identify with the life-giving properties of the Egyptian god Osiris, or the fertility and abundance of a mother-goddess such as Isis or Demeter. The symbols adorning the walls of the chamber, and also the garments worn during the ritual, will reflect the purpose at hand. The concept underlying all forms of 'high magic' is to lift one's perspective from a domestic level to a domain that is archetypal; to shift one's field of awareness from the mundane to the cosmic. William Butler Yeats, a wonderfully gifted poet who was also a ritual occultist, alludes to this in his descriptions of the 'temple of the Alchemical Rose'. Here, with his imagination inflamed by ritual, each petal in the Rosicrucian Rose seemed to be transformed 'into the likeness of Living Beings of extraordinary beauty'. When he turned to the pillars of Horus, each appeared to be 'a column of...shapes, divinities, it seemed of the wind, who in a whirling dance of more than human vehemence, rose playing upon pipes and cymbals; and from among these shapes were thrust out hands, and in these hands were censers. I was bid place my censer also in a hand and take my place and dance.'[10]

Humility

It also has to be said that vain human strivings for the greater mystical reality beyond can bring its own range of problems. If the quest is solely for personal fulfilment, rather than a humble desire for greater self-knowledge in the service of others, then there may well be the flaw of ego in the outcome. Within the ranks of mystics and esotericists, ritual occultists have been particularly prone to excesses of ego. In the ceremonial approach it has been all too common for magicians to emerge from their encounters with the Osiris-energy, or the Isis-energy, and then take their ritually enlarged egos out into the world at large, subsequently engaging in power-play with their followers or neophytes. Similarly, several of the more flamboyant contemporary eastern gurus have been known to use their 'spiritual' charisma to dominate compliant followers.

At the same time, it is of little communal benefit if, in pursuing a spiritual path, so much time is spent within an ashram or spiritual retreat that one's inner attentiveness renders one unable to operate in a meaningful way in the outside world later on. The task is surely to assimilate the profound experiences of the Greater Mystery within the context of familiar reality, to bring greater vision into our everyday lives.

Humility is an appropriate state of mind for this endeavour, whatever spiritual traditions or practices we may follow, and regardless of our degree of apparent social or business 'success' in in the secular world.

Many who meditate, pray or use visualization techniques find that these types of activities enrich their personal lives, and a sense of humility reminds us of our inevitable 'smallness' in the grand scheme of things. For, as mentioned earlier, we can simply hope to experience infinity at the edge: the vast cosmic ocean lies beyond, and within, in all directions.

Humility means recognizing the limitations of our perspective, while opening ourselves to the vast possibilities that exist along the spectrum of consciousness. As soon as we begin to take pride in our accomplishments - however great - we are really closing ourselves off to something greater still. Arrogance and pride are states of mind which produce a type of boundary mentality in which the person demarcates himself from others who are in turn perceived as inferior because of their lack of comparable attainments or possessions. Seen in this way, arrogance is an attitude of being closed and rigid, while humility is a state of openness. Similarly, if we over-value our material possessions and focus inordinately on our external social persona, it is inevitable that the inner perspective will suffer as a consequence.

With these perspectives in mind, then, the exploration of inner states of awareness assumes vital importance. All mystical and religious traditions agree that it is in the inner world of the spirit where the real insights lie, where our dreams and visions first take form. Jesus himself reminded us of this when he said: 'The Kingdom of God is within...'

And so we must turn our attention to what I would like to call the visionary landscape. This has very much to do with the geography of consciousness, the mapping of the inner terrain of the human imagination.

3.

The Visionary Landscape

The visionary landscape has many levels. It can be a domain characterized by a sense of Infinite Space and profound meaning beyond manifested form; it can be a world permeated by vivid light and sacred imagery; it can be a realm of nature spirits, *devas* and faery beings, and it can be a world populated by terrifying, bestial energy forms which seem to have arisen from the grossest levels of existence. However, being a *visionary* means seeing things in a more complete way - penetrating the veils that engulf us all, and experiencing an ever-broader spectrum of experiential reality.

There are, of course, numerous dimensions to the visionary universe and it is simplistic to conceive of it simply in terms of light and transcendence. If there is a polarity to our very being, as Carl Jung has suggested, if indeed we all dwell in psychic spaces characterized by varying degrees of integration and chaos, of good and evil, of transcendence and debasement, then the journey into altered states of consciousness will surely reveal all of these at different times in our lives. Accordingly, visionary literature and art - tangible manifestations of the inner world - similarly reveal a multi-dimensional psyche, an inner terrain that at different times is mysterious, miraculous, transformative and, on some occasions, profoundly confronting.

Writers, artists, musicians - creators who open themselves to their psychic energies - manifest in their work the contents of their visions: emotions, thoughts and perceptions. Their art becomes a map of personal and transpersonal consciousness, a frozen image of an ever-changing inner world. And so the mystic path, the path of self-exploration, the journey towards transcendence, takes us through an extraordinarily diverse maze of images towards the Greater Mystery which lies beyond all forms. It is a journey towards, and beyond, the light; a journey towards what we can only allude to as the core reality, the highest state of consciousness.

Instinctively, we conceive of this mystic journey as leading from darkness into light, since this is a metaphor which helps us appreciate the quest for self-knowledge. We gradually emerge, layer by layer, from the darkness of our ignorance, transcending each level in the hope that beyond will lie the light of new meaning.

The visionary terrain requires a geography for all of these levels of exploration, and in different traditions of art and religion we find reflections of each of these domains in turn. And it is always necessary to remember that as spirit descends into form, as it were, it gives rise to a vast range of archetypal symbols and metaphors - all subsequently shaped by culture and language. It is beyond these mythic images that the most profound level of visionary consciousness is reached.

Cosmic Consciousness

Cosmic consciousness, from the viewpoint of our limited human perspective, seems to be the highest state of consciousness that can be attained - a level that Robert de Ropp has called 'objective consciousness'.[1] R.M. Bucke, the Canadian psychiatrist whose core mystical experience inspired William James, referred to cosmic consciousness as a 'consciousness of the Cosmos, that is, of the life and order of the Universe'. Bucke describes how he came to experience this state of realization as follows:

> I was in a state of quiet, almost passive enjoyment, not actually thinking, but letting ideas, images, and emotions flow of themselves through my mind. All at once, without any warning of any kind, I found myself wrapped in a flame-coloured cloud. For an instant I thought of fire, an immense conflagration somewhere close by in that great city; the next I knew the fire was within myself. Directly afterward there came upon me a sense of exultation, of immense joyousness accompanied or immediately followed by an intellectual

> illumination impossible to describe. Among other things, I did not merely come to believe, but I saw that the universe is not composed of dead matter, but is, on the contrary a living Presence; I became conscious in myself of eternal life.[2]

Bucke was for a number of years the superintendent at a mental hospital in London, Ontario, and he experienced his spontaneous mystical experience when he was thirty-five years old. For the rest of his life he pondered its significance, finally publishing his famous book on comparative mysticism in 1901. In *Cosmic Consciousness*, Bucke put forward the view that it was this state of mystical illumination that characterized the great religious leaders in history. He came to the view that 'the human race, having evolved from "simple consciousness" to "self consciousness", was destined to continue evolving into cosmic consciousness, which an elite vanguard, including great religious leaders like Buddha, Jesus Christ and Muhammad had already attained.'[3]

In Eastern yogic mysticism the concept of cosmic consciousness is given the name *samadhi*: it is a state beyond name and form and to this extent is virtually indescribable. Pancham Sinh noted in his *Hatha Yoga Pradipka* translation:

> The whole of this world and all the schemes of the mind are but the creatures of thought. Discarding these thoughts and taking leave of all conjectures, obtain peace. As camphor disappears in fire, and rock salt in water, so the mind united with *atma* loses its identity. All that appears is the knowable, the mind is called knowledge. When the knowable and the knowledge are both destroyed equally, then duality is destroyed.[4]

Theos Bernard, in his *Hatha Yoga* provided a further commentary:

> *Samadhi* cannot be experienced until a condition of mindlessness has been created. All modifications of the thinking principle must cease: all thought forms must be removed, yet some form of awareness must remain. Without yoga experience it is difficult to imagine what is meant; that is why teachers do not even try to explain.[5]

However, one figure who was keen to explain the inexplicable was Alan Watts, the well-known British writer on Zen Buddhism and mysticism who became a pioneering figure in the American Human Potential Movement. Watts, like many of his generation, had been inspired by R.M. Bucke and he endeavoured to explain what he meant by cosmic consciousness in his autobiographical essay, *This is It*. Here Watts described two of his personal mystical experiences:

> Shortly after I had first begun to study Indian and Chinese philosophy I was sitting one night by the fire, trying to make out what was the right attitude of mind for meditation as it is practised in Hindu and Buddhist disciplines. It seemed to me that several attitudes were possible, but as they appeared mutually exclusive and contradictory I was trying to fit them into one – all to no purpose. Finally, in sheer disgust, I decided to reject them all and to have no special attitude of mind whatsoever. In the force of throwing them away it seemed that I threw myself away as well, for quite suddenly the weight of my own body disappeared. I felt that I owned nothing, not even a self, and that nothing owned me. The whole world became as transparent and unobstructed as my own mind; the 'problem of life' simply ceased to exist, and for about eighteen hours I and everything around me felt like the wind blowing leaves across a field on an autumn day.

His second experience came a few years later:

> I had been attempting to practise what Buddhists call 'recollection' (*smriti*) or constant awareness of the immediate present...Someone suggested that there was no need for such effort since 'we are always completely *in* the present' regardless of our thoughts. This, actually quite obvious, remark again brought on the sudden sensation of having no weight.
>
> At the same time, the present seemed to become a kind of moving stillness, an eternal stream from which neither I nor anything could deviate. I saw that everything, just as it is now, is IT – is the whole point of there being life and a universe. I saw that when the *Upanishads* said 'That art Thou!' or 'All the world is Brahman', they meant just exactly what they said. Each thing, each event, each experience in its inescapable nowness and in all its own particular

> individuality was precisely what it should be, and so much so that it acquired a divine authority and originality.[6]

Of course, these types of realizations have occurred throughout history. William Blake (1757–1827), in his immortal phrase, that 'If the doors of perception were cleansed, everything would appear to man as it is, infinite', and Thomas Traherne (1636–74) made much the same point when he observed that 'the world is a mirror of Infinite Beauty, yet no man sees it. It is a Temple of Majesty, yet no man regards it.'

The medieval Dominican monk Henry Suso (1295–1366) was acknowledging the reality of Cosmic Unity when he wrote: 'All creatures have existed eternally in the divine essence...So far as they are in God, they are the same life, the same essence, the same power, the same One, and nothing less.'[7]

So what we are talking of in the experience of cosmic consciousness is essentially a state of oneness with the universe, the profound realization that all aspects of creation are interconnected and flow from the same Infinite Source.

The state of being which exists beyond form is, however, necessarily incapable of description through words and images. Mystics have called it 'ineffable' for this reason, and we can only allude to it with metaphors. Mahayana Buddhists thus talk of *Sunyata*, the Universal Void, while Jewish Kabbalists refer to *Ain Soph Aur*, the Limitless Light. These days transpersonal psychologists refer to the Unity Experience and mean very much the same thing. Cosmic consciousness is the supreme experience in the mystical traditions – the complete transcendence of duality. As Alan Watts so aptly put it: this is IT.

However, if mystical transcendence defies description, less exalted regions of the cosmological landscape reveal themselves through images and archetypes that are more accessible. In visionary art, mythology and cosmology we find characteristic themes that reveal different dimensions of the mind and spirit.

Art and the Inner World

Throughout history there have been visionary artists whose work has revealed aspects of the mythic imagination: these have been the artists intent on proceeding beyond familiar reality and drawing for their inspiration on the realms of inner space.

Although such a subject could fill many volumes in itself, it is useful briefly to consider the visionary world manifested through art, for here are tangible depictions of man's experience of the archetypal worlds.

Leonardo da Vinci once said that 'where the spirit does not work with the hand there is no art', and Marcel Brion has similarly articulated the role of the artist as a visionary:

> A visionary is a man who sees beneath the surface of things; no obstacle can block the path of his perception; he is the discoverer of dizzying crystalline heights, the chronicling of unknown worlds. He is capable of conjuring treacherous Hell itself into submission, of keeping the supernatural and the natural in equipoise; like Moses he casts himself down at the threshold of Mystery, trembling indeed, yet sure of himself as seer and master.[8]

Not surprisingly, we find in visionary art all the elements which make up the spectrum of awareness culminating in mystical self-realization: an encounter with the depths of the soul, depictions of primal and sacred images, and pathways through to transcendence.

One of Albrecht Dürer's characteristic woodcuts from his Apocalypse series, completed around 1498, shows the celestial domain clearly differentiated from the material and human world of suffering and anguish. It also depicts the eternal struggle between the opposing forces of good and evil, symbolized here by the angelic sun and demonic moon. Christ is shown midway between the two – a mediator between humanity and heaven.

Another interesting artistic composition from this era, *The Temptation of St Anthony* by Martin Schongauer (1445–91), shows St Anthony attacked by myriad demons and devils during his ascent to heaven. A drypoint etching admired by Michelangelo, this work reveals aspects of the religious imagination that we will find time and again, both in art and cosmology: here the demons and devils are composites of various bestial forms blended together in a menacing way – lions' heads, talons, hawks' beaks, horns, spikes and reptilean features combine here, as they do in parallel works by Hieronymus Bosch, into surreal projections of the lower animal self.

Bosch produced his own version of *The Temptation of St*

Anthony around 1505, and included in his painting a bizarre array of bird-animal combinations and human figures caught up in a quagmire of nightmare imagery. However, Bosch had a profoundly spiritual side too, as seen in the idyllic *Garden of Earthly Delights*. Here are images of Christ with Adam and Eve in a fantasy garden centred on a mythic fountain of life. Bosch is thought to have been influenced by the Adamic sect which venerated Adam's nakedness as an expression of divine innocence. His paintings often show a dynamic interplay between the forces of human degradation and mystical transcendence.

It is always interesting to consider how artists make leaps into the imagination, for this provides a clue to the states of consciousness accessed through their creativity.

William Blake (1757–1827) had visions even when he was a child. At the age of four he said he saw God looking through his window, and when he was nine he saw 'a tree filled with angels, bright angelic wings bespangling every bough, like stars'. Blake's paintings throng with celestial and spiritual beings, and he was certainly influenced by his knowledge of such mystical and esoteric writers as Jakob Boehme, Swedenborg, Agrippa von Nettesheim and Paracelsus. But he also drew directly from his visionary experience. With his friend John Varley he held seances in London, where he claimed to converse with demons in prose, and with angels in poetic verse. In a series of meticulous pencil drawings he described exactly what he saw in his spirit-vision. Blake also created a cosmology of his own – encompassing the four Zoas, or 'Mighty Ones' that he said resided in every person: *Tharmas*, the physical body or senses; *Luvah*, the emotions, especially love; *Urthona*, the creative imagination, which he equated with the Holy Spirit; and *Urizen*, reason – corresponding to Satan, or the 'fall' of divine essence. Although Blake's vision is often menacing and confronting, he believed in mankind's essential sacredness. For him there were clear signs of the eternal in all things:

To see a World in a Grain of Sand
And a Heaven in a Wild Flower,
Hold infinity in the palm of your hand
And Eternity in an hour.

Closer to our own time, the visionary perspective in art is well represented by the mythic directions within Surrealism and the Ars Phantastica School of Vienna.

The Surrealists sought to make the inner world tangible through their art, their paintings and writings endeavouring to fuse dream and reality. Influenced by founder André Breton, several of the more 'free-form' Surrealists sought in automatic writing and spontaneous forms of art a means of overcoming the limitations of the intellectual mind and tapping the realm of creative inspiration direct. In a manner not unlike isolating oneself in a cave or float tank, they tried, as Anna Balakian has commented, 'by placing themselves in a state of stupefying attentiveness...to shut out all outside disturbances and to give free play to the inner powers of association of words and images which these suggested...'[9]

Wolfgang Paalen, an Austrian Surrealist who lived for a time in Mexico, developed a technique known as *fumage*. He would hold canvases freshly coated with oil paint above a candle so that the smoke would trace eerie random patterns in the wet paint. He would then overlay these images with surreal, supranormal detail, as in his work of 1938, *Conflict of the Principles of Darkness*. Similarly, Max Ernst – arguably the most visionary of all the Surrealists – developed the process of *frottage* to stimulate the inner workings of the mind. In this technique Ernst would rub lightly with pencil upon the sheets of paper placed on his floor boards, thus allowing the uneven surface to come through on his paper as a texture. When he looked carefully at his *frottages* he found a mystical process coming into play. 'When gazing at these drawings,' he wrote, 'I was surprised at the sudden intensification of my visionary faculties and at the hallucinatory succession of contradictory images being superimposed on each other.'[10]

In 1926, meanwhile, Yves Tanguy produced a series of automatic drawings, scratchings, arabesques, loops and tufts, which, when transferred to a canvas coated with colour, seemed to produce 'a universe of smoke, brushwood and ghosts, which defy gravity'. Tanguy was interesting for another reason as well. Many of his paintings are grey and eerie, like landscapes of the nether world. As a youth Tanguy used to dive into the sea in search of bones and pebbles washed by the waves, and there is a strong sense in his paintings of an ocean of hidden images, of forms about to manifest from a more ethereal essence. Later his pupil, Roberto Matta, used surreal techniques of automatic painting to produce a series of paintings he called 'psychological morphologies'. These were characterized by a remarkable sense of freedom, the spontaneous use of colour, and the exploration of cosmic realities beyond the ego.

More recently still, the Ars Phantastica School of art has flourished in Vienna, including within its ranks such painters as Anton Lehmden, Helmuth Leherb, Rudolf Hausner, Eric Brauer and Ernst Fuchs. These artists, too, have explored different dimensions of the visionary terrain, their art thronging with mystical and hallucinatory images.

Of these artists, Ernst Fuchs is, to my mind, the most interesting, for his cosmological paintings are perhaps the most impressive portrayals of the polarities of the inner world since those of Hieronymus Bosch. As Marcel Brion has said of his art: 'Rising from nocturnal darkness and the twisting paths of the deepest unconscious, Fuchs' creatures force us under the spell of that reality to which there is no access except in a visionary state.'

As a child, Fuchs was absorbed by imaginative stories read to him by his father: 'Thus I was introduced into the realm of faerie, the world of elves and mermaids, noble dragon slayers, heroes and titans, dwarfs and sprites. The bulges and hollows of my featherbed were metamorphosed into the snowy summits or gloomy caves of imaginary mountain ranges, increasingly populated with all those beings that are to this day the subjects of my art.'[11]

Later, when he began to establish himself as a painter in the mid-1940s, he came to see the creative process, as the Surrealists had done before him, as a type of channelling process:

> I noticed for the first time how obsessed I was with my creative urge, as if possessed by a medium. My hand, moving as if in a trance, created the inexplicable. In a few days I created a large number of delicate line drawings...By way of these drawings I rapidly moved away from my earliest models and plunged into the yet unknown depths of my imagination.[12]

Fuchs' most dramatic work, which combines stylistic tendencies borrowed from the Old Masters with symbolic motifs taken from Jewish *Merkabah* mysticism and more recently Christianity, have their source, as he says, 'in the desire to create a means of transcending time, entering eternity'. Fuchs believes that art is really akin to visionary meditation.

> We should all learn to contemplate images again... for it is in images that the language of the spirits, the messages from Heaven, manifest themselves, as they did in the tongues of the prophets... The image gives free play to our dreams.[13]

Archetypes and Cosmologies

As we can see from both the mystical origins of religious experience and the various approaches to visionary art, the inner landscape of the psyche appears to present itself on a number of different levels, or tiers, that extend from our known world of everyday reality into the far reaches of inner space, eventually tapering off into infinity. So the Jewish Kabbalists spoke of a Ladder of Lights extending up to heaven, and the Gnostics and Neoplatonists of a series of 'emanations' reaching from the Infinite Light down to the world of humankind.

It seems that our minds structure the inner universe so that if we are to consider the psyche as a type of metaphorical map, transcendence lies in an 'upward' direction. The distinguished psychotherapist Eugene Caslant began to explore guided imagery in the 1930s – a precursor to the 'creative visualization' exercises that are now part of the New Consciousness – and he came to the view that to ascend in the imagination seemed to produce a feeling of tranquillity and self-composure. He therefore proposed specific 'symbols of ascent' for use in meditation, and these included a ladder, a staircase and a flying chariot. Following on from this, Caslant's pupil, Robert Desoille, developed the idea of the 'directed daydream' in which he could lead his patients through encounters with archetypal images.

Desoille confirmed that 'upward' meditation led to feelings of lightness and euphoria, while to travel 'downwards' could produce feelings of anxiety and fear associated with the perception of darkness. Desoille's view, though, was that one should not draw away from these domains through fear, but should meet them head-on:

> The patient must learn to control the 'archetypes' within himself, to be free from them, and thereby lose his fear of them...The goal of the technique is to direct the patient towards the fulfilment of his human potentialities through the creative development of man's basic biological impulses into a higher and harmonic idea.

The visionary landscape throngs with archetypes – the spiritual energies of the psyche. Carl Jung believed that the archetypes were part of the collective unconscious – a level of the mind which represented, in symbolic form, 'the constantly repeated experiences of humanity'. But he also believed that the archetypes appeared to lead their own independent existence, appearing in visions and dreams in a way that invariably had a profound spiritual impact on the recipient. So for Jung, and for others who have similarly studied the dynamics of the deep levels of the psyche, angels, archangels, 'principalities and powers' and other types of intermediary spiritual beings are all examples of archetypal consciousness breaking through into more familiar levels of awareness. As Jung himself observed, the archetype contained such power that it could 'seize hold of the psyche with a kind of primeval force'.

Seen in this way, cosmologies are maps of archetypal states of consciousness. As Jung's colleague, Jolande Jacobi, has written:

> We find the archetypes recurring in all mythologies, fairy tales, religious traditions and mysteries. What are the myths of the 'night sea journey', of the 'wandering hero' or of the sea monster, if not the eternal knowledge of the sun's setting and rebirth, transformed into images? Prometheus the Stealer of Fire, Heracles the dragon slayer, the countless creation myths, the fall from paradise, the mysteries of creation, the virgin birth, the treacherous betrayal of the hero, the dismembering of Osiris, and many other myths and fairy tales represent psychic processes in symbolic images. Similarly, the figures of the snakes, the fish, the sphinx, the helpful animals, the Tree of the World, the Great Mother, the enchanted prince, the *puer aeternus*, the Mage, the Wise

> Man, Paradise etc. stand for certain motifs and contents of the collective unconscious. In every single individual psyche they can awaken new life, exert their magic power and condense it into a kind of 'individual mythology'...the archetypes taken as a whole represent the sum of the latent potentialities of the human psyche – a vast store of ancestral knowledge about the profound relations between God, Man and Cosmos...'[14]

Cosmologies also have a structure which provides them with much more than intellectual relevance. There is invariably a path into the cosmic realm – through a secret door, an entrance in a rock, or 'the crack between the worlds' (as in the Yaqui accounts of Carlos Casteneda), and this takes us into mythic space. Thus in Greek mythology, Persephone was snatched by Aidoneus (Hades) from the Nysian plain where she was picking flowers, and taken down into the underworld. Zeus sent Hermes to the underworld to restore her to life but because Persephone had eaten a pomegranate seed given to her by Hades, she was destined to dwell in an endless transition between the worlds of the living and the dead.

However, from the viewpoint of exploring the visionary landscape, we can consider the Underworld not as a land of the 'dead' so much as a realm of awareness buried or repressed from consciousness – a domain of forgotten dreams, latencies and potentials. It is the depths of the mind that have to be brought into awareness. Jung believed implicitly in the value of working with the dark or neglected side of the mind (the Shadow) as a path towards greater self-knowledge. As mentioned earlier, transcendence is all about passing through darkness to the light – and beyond.

Cosmologies are maps that point in the direction of transcendence, and we often find that the 'founder gods' of creation in different religions – for example, the ancient Greek Kronos and his Roman counterpart Saturn – are so far removed from the domain of the familiar world that they have little contact with everyday affairs, and few descriptive qualities are ascribed to them. This in turn reflects their transcendent qualities. The universe, if it is perceived to be 'governed' at all, is managed by lesser deities like Zeus, Jupiter and Yahweh: these are lordly or tribal intermediaries, positioned on a level midway between humankind and the Greater Mystery beyond.

So if we look at the cosmological map that characterized ancient Greek religion we find that Kronos, the god of time, was believed to have existed prior to the creation of the world. He was later deposed by one of his children, Zeus, who thus gained supremacy over the manifested world of form. Zeus, as 'father of the gods', was perceived as ruler of heaven and earth, and we can interpret this to mean that in the ancient Greek psyche he was the dominant archetype. He was capable of changing into different forms – a satyr, a white bull, a swan, a shower of gold – and he also caused the thunderbolts that were believed to cause storms and death.

While Kronos was remote, Zeus was very tangible: he had seven wives and embroiled himself in numerous romances, and the oak tree and eagle were sacred to him. However, these descriptive qualities by definition place him at a lower level in the cosmological framework. He was a god with whom ordinary Greeks could identify (he was at times very human!), and they could also 'look up' to him. But beyond Zeus, in the further reaches of space, lay the mythic origins of the creation itself.

If Zeus is an archetypal 'father' god, we find counterparts for him in Jupiter (ancient Rome) and the sun-god Ra (ancient Egypt) and in their 'Mother' goddess equivalents: Rhea, Ops (or Magna Mater) and Hathor. All of these ancient pantheons had a rich diversity of lesser gods and goddesses populating the spectrum between the divine and familiar worlds.

This is not to say that all cosmologies present an appealing hierarchy. The Gnostic sects regarded the world as intrinsically evil, since it was so far removed from the Spirit, and their lesser heavens were often populated by entities that could potentially bar one's spiritual progress. The third-century Ophites, for example, conceived of a lower heavenly domain inhabited by seven obstructive animal demons: Michael (a lion), Souriel (a bull), Raphael (a hissing snake), Gabriel (an eagle), Thauthabaoth (a bear), Erathaoth (a dog) and Oneol or Thartharaoth (an ass).

The Christian theologian, Origen, described in his *Contra Celsum* how the Ophites addressed these seven bestial demons on their inner journeys of the spirit. The dialogue ran: 'Hail you solitary King, Bond of Invisibility, First Power, guarded by the spirit of Foreknowledge and by Wisdom. From this place I am sent on, pure, already a part of the light of Son and Father. Let grace be with me, yes Father, let it be with me.' Having conquered the demon through this formula, and by appealing to God on high, the mystic's soul was now able to proceed to the more lofty heavens.

In general the Gnostics believed that these heavens (called aeons or 'eternities' because they were outside space and time) were emanations from a first principle which might be visualized as vibrant energy. The first aeons were pure and perfect in themselves, but as they reached down, closer and closer to the level we call reality, they became tainted by contact with the world. All material things were regarded as basically deficient because they were only dim reflections of the divine. In fact, because the earth was created out of chaos, which the Gnostics believed to be devoid of cosmic energy, the 'deficiencies' came to be equated with negativity, or evil. Some Gnostics also believed that when the soul fell into matter from its earlier elevated state, it became sorrowful because physical existence involved suffering. And like Gautama Buddha, these Gnostics equated suffering with ignorance. The path of self-knowledge eliminated ignorance and suffering and led to spiritual renewal: body became spirit, evil transmuted itself into good. The Gnostics thus saw their prime task as gaining personal knowledge (*gnosis*) of the higher spiritual realms. To this extent they were very much the forerunners of the Human Potential Movement today.

Heaven and Hell

The most extreme polarities of archetypal imagery occur in cosmological concepts relating to an afterlife. For if we accept a belief system (as in Christianity and the ancient Egyptian religion) that brings with it the concept of a post-mortem judgement, then it follows that our destiny, following death, must be quite clear-cut: to ascend into heaven or descend into hell.

According to Christian belief, Jesus came into the world to bring salvation from evil and death, and to provide assurance of an afterlife of eternal happiness for all who believed in him. It was also assumed by the early Christians, and is still accepted by some Christian fundamentalists today, that those not finding salvation in Christ would be consigned to hell.

The actual concept of hell seems to have derived from the Jewish idea of Gehenna (*Ge Hinnom*) - a valley in Palestine where the Israelites sacrificed their children to Moloch, God of the Ammonites. Gehenna came to be regarded as a place of torment and abomination and the hell-fire imagery reflects the fact that the Valley of Hinnom was a place where refuse was discarded and fires lit to avoid the spread of deadly disease. All of these factors were subsequently compounded into the 'bottomless pit of eternal fire' where the wicked were said to be punished when they died.

Christ was expected by the early Christians to return in glory, and at this time devout followers would be taken up to heaven. The earliest Christians felt, in fact, that they would not experience normal death - for the second coming was imminent. When it failed to materialize quite so soon, however, the first Christians came to regard the physical life as a testing ground where the decision for Christ could be made, and this idea still continues today. Martyrs and other 'good' Christians would go straight to heaven, while unbelievers and the wicked would go instead to hell.

The idea of an intermediate state, purgatory, where sinful Christians could be cleansed of their sins prior to entering paradise developed later, and was not actually enunciated until 1254. According to this belief, Christian souls would pass from purgatory to paradise at the final judgement, now clearly to be expected some time in the future. Jesus himself seems not to have held this belief, however, since at the crucifixion he promised the penitent thief: 'Truly, I say to you, today you will be with me in Paradise.'

The popular Christian concept of heaven was certainly influenced by Old Testament references to God's Garden of Eden - a cool leafy paradise where fine trees grew, watered by the fountain of life. St Peter is said to have had a visionary glimpse of a similar paradise: a world filled with radiant light, beautiful flowers and fruit, where the dead - in shining clothes - intermingled with the angels. Later, however, theologians began to differentiate between heaven and paradise, defining heaven as a metaphysical state where saints, angels and apostles resided in rapt contemplation of God the Father, Son and Holy Ghost.

Hell, though, was always a grim place indeed, as any perusal of medieval Christian art will confirm. In the Byzantine rendering of the last judgement in the mosaic west wall of Torcello (twelfth century), we see burning wheels below Christ's feet, issuing a fiery stream that leads down into hell, while in the Psalter of St Louis (mid-thirteenth century), the damned are trapped in the gaping jaws of hell.

The distinction between paradise and damnation is also developed in ancient Egyptian cosmology, and it appears that the Egyptians were the first to conceive of a post-mortem judgement. Their cosmology is described in several Books of the Dead, including *The Theban Recension of the Book of the Dead*, *The Book of Gates* and *The Book of the Am-Tuat*. These books were compiled and transcribed onto papyrus in the New Kingdom (1580–1370 BC) and describe the passage of the deceased soul through the Tuat or underworld.

Some of these books emphasize resurrection – where the faithful followers of Osiris spend their days after death tilling the Elysian Fields – while other texts describe a process where deceased souls travel in the company of the Sun God on a continuous cycle of daily rebirth. The concept of judgement is especially emphasized in the Osirian texts where, depending on the verdict at the weighing of the deceased person's heart in the Hall of Judgement, the individual either entered the Elysian Fields or was led off to hideous destruction.

In developing their religious cosmology, the ancient Egyptians had observed the passage of the sun across the sky each day and its consequent setting in the west, and formed the belief that the night-land was the abode of the dead. The dead became known as the 'dwellers in the west' and entry to the other world was through Manu, the Mountain of the Sunset – which lay on the west bank of the Nile.

In another sense, the Tuat was also on the plane of the earth itself – in a counterpart of Upper and Lower Egypt in which the twelve hours of darkness corresponded to different regions of the kingdom. For example, in the *Am-Tuat*, the first division beyond the entry chamber corresponded to Abydos, and there were subsequent divisions which related to the desert regions around Memphis ruled by Seker, the delta districts of Busiris and Mendes ruled by Osiris, and the city of Heliopolis ruled by Annu (Temu-Khepera-Ra).

The deceased person, in mummified form, entered the Tuat in a boat and for the most part journeyed with Ra along a mighty river. However in some parts of the Tuat the river disappeared altogether and the journey was across treacherous, snake-ridden deserts: it finally culminated in passage through the body of a giant serpent.

Osiris, in his role as Lord of the Dead, was widely considered to be the archetype for all deceased souls, and sections of the Tuat were ruled by him. Indeed, some of the dead earned the right – through their purity and good deeds on earth – to live in his kingdom. Here they were nourished by barley cakes, bread and beer, and worked the Field of Earu in the same way that they had tilled the pastures of the Nile during their lives on earth. Other deceased souls spent eternity traversing the heavens with Ra, welcomed by the gods and, according to the texts, regarded as their equals.

As with the Christian depictions of hell, though, the various Books of the Dead also describe the grim fate that was likely to befall the impure and wicked, and the Tuat was no place to be cast aside. As the noted translator of so many ancient Egyptian texts, Sir Wallis Budge, comments:

> In all the Books of the Other World we find pits of fire, abysses of darkness, murderous knives, streams of boiling water, foul stenches, fiery serpents, hideous animal-headed monsters and creatures, and cruel, death-dealing beings of various shapes...[15]

The Egyptian Books of the Dead, though, have an important cosmological counterpart in the Tibetan Book of the Dead or *Bardo Thodol* which describes different phases of the post-mortem existence. Of all cosmological systems of this type, it would appear – for reasons which will be discussed later – to have the most relevance in the mapping of altered states of consciousness in relation to the experience of death. The book provides an account of the different *bardo* visions through which deceased individuals pass, and these visions consist of the symbolic effect of the person's own *karma* – good and evil deeds – and the nature of the personality. The Tibetan lamas have for centuries taught a technique of dying that enables the individual to pass through the *bardo* visions and thereby enter the transcendent state of Nirvana.

The *Bardo Thodol* begins with the loftiest experience of all cosmic consciousness. Here it is called the Clear Light of Illumination, and it is experienced as the beholder loses his own ego in favour of the Void. This is a state of transcendent unity with the Oneness of the cosmos, a state of sublime liberation from the constrictions of the sensory world.

According to the *Bardo Thodol* many individuals nevertheless find that they cannot sustain the experience of the Clear Light, so at this point there dawns the Secondary Clear Light which occurs at a mystical level where the beholder is illuminated in an ecstasy of wave energy flow. If he rides with the flow he may sustain this state of consciousness but should he attempt to control it, this in itself would indicate an act of ego, and he would necessarily fall away from the Unity Experience. This being so, the individual would now descend into what are referred to in the *Bardo Thodol* as the *Chonyid Bardo*, or karmic hallucinatory realms.

This *bardo* equates with the archetypal and cosmological levels of consciousness which have been described earlier. In this *bardo*, as one writer has succinctly expressed it, 'any and every shape - human, divine, diabolical, heroic, evil, animal, thing - which the human brain conjured up or the past life recalls, can present itself to consciousness; shapes and forms and sounds whirling by endlessly.'[16]

It was in this phase that the Tibetans believed they would encounter the Seven Peaceful Deities and the Seven Visions of the Wrathful Deities incorporating fifty-eight embodiments of the human personality couched within traditional, culturally delineated forms and shapes. These, together with lower grades of forces and potencies, constitute the Tibetan pantheon. As the noted compiler and editor of *The Tibetan Book of the Dead*, W.Y. Evans-Wentz comments:

> The chief deities themselves are the embodiments of universal divine forces, with which the deceased is inseparably related, for through him, as being the microcosm of the macrocosm, penetrate all impulses and forces, good and bad alike. Samanta-Bhadra, the All-Good, thus personified Reality, the Primordial Clear Light of the Unborn, Unshaped *Dharma-Kaya*. Vairochana is the Originator of all phenomena, the Cause of all Causes. As the

> Universal Father, Vairochana manifests or spreads forth as seed, or semen, all things; his *shakti*, the Mother of Great Space, is the Universal Womb into which the seed falls and evolves as the world-systems. Vajra-Sattva symbolises Immutability. Ratna-Sambhaba is the Beautifier, the Source of all Beauty in the Universe. Amitabha is Infinite Compassion and Love Divine, the *Christos*. Amogha-Siddhi is the personification of Almighty Power or Omnipotence. And the minor deities, heroes, *dakinis* (or 'fairies'), goddesses, lords of death, *rakshasas*, demons, spirits, and all others, correspond to definite human thoughts, passions and impulses, high and low, human and sub-human and super-human, in *karmic* form, as they take shape from the seeds of thought forming in the percipient's consciousness-content.[17]

The third phase, or *Sidpa Bardo*, is the period of 're-entry' where the individual who has not managed to transcend the cosmic imagery is drawn down into rebirth. However, the Tibetan Buddhists emphasize that liberation *is* possible – one does not have to return to further cycles of incarnation. Quite simply, our quality of consciousness decides that for us.

Basically what the Tibetans call the 'Great Liberation' is achieved by ego-loss or 'death of the ego', and, as we have seen, this state may be achieved immediately after death, in the first *bardo* of the Clear Light. It is also possible if one is able to transcend the images of the deities who appear in the second *bardo*. However, below these levels the ego gains more and more strength, and seeks 'rebirth' in the world of the senses, where it is able to assert itself once more as dominant. In this way, according to the Tibetan Buddhists, the cycles of incarnation continue to perpetuate themselves.

So where does this leave us? Are we to believe the after-death scenarios of Christian scripture or the cosmology outlined by the ancient Egyptians? Or are we, instead, to take as our guide the heavenly emanations of the Gnostics or *The Tibetan Book of the Dead*?

As I mentioned earlier, it seems to me that we do not have to make a choice in favour of any specific belief system in our investigation of visionary states of consciousness. Belief systems and cosmologies provide us with *detail* only – vast and complex assortments of sundry gods and goddesses, pantheons of angels and devils – and these in turn reflect the world-view of a given culture. We have seen, for example, how the Christian notion of hell-fire derived originally from the bonfires of *Ge Hinnom* and how the Egyptian underworld was populated by a composite of all the worst things the local inhabitants could possibly imagine: pits of fire, hideous animal-headed monsters and dangerous serpents.

These images are important, of course, as examples of symbols that have seeped into the psyche of a culture, appearing within its belief system. However, they are not part of the visionary process itself. The latter is much more direct, and in a sense quite uncomplicated. Cosmic consciousness seems to break through only when we let go of the detail, transcend our belief systems, eliminate the domestic programming and doctrinal boundaries which constrict us, and open ourselves to the overriding Oneness that subsumes all diversity. We saw this in the spontaneous experiences of Alan Watts and R.M. Bucke and in the remarkable insight of Henry Suso,and it is implicit in the open-ended frameworks of spiritual consciousness proposed by Mahayana Buddhism, the Kabbalah and Gnosticism.

All cosmologies, all frameworks of consciousness – whether we are talking about *bardo* levels, the Tree of Life reaching up to *Ain Soph Aur* or emanations from the First Aeon – are metaphors which describe the awesome range of psychic imagery which lies between the world of individual perception and the Infinite Void beyond form. The gulf between our ego-based realities and complete transcendence is populated by personifications of our fears, aspirations, hopes and dreams: by our visions and our nightmares. The more profound of these, the more awesome ones, are the archetypes of the collective unconscious, which appear to us clothed in the vestments of our culture. But beyond them still further, beyond belief systems and cosmologies, we move towards the Greater Mystery itself.

The challenge for our present times – an era which some feel to be at 'the end of history' – is to accept that our earlier doctrinal belief systems have become outmoded and incomplete. At a time when transpersonal research, parapsychology, quantum physics and medical technology are providing new insights into consciousness itself, we find ourselves requiring more expansive frameworks of reality –

frameworks that can be validated by personal experience rather than rest on faith or belief alone. It is to them that we now turn.

4.

Dimensions of the Paranormal

Western civilization brings with it a certain arrogance of perception – we have developed an almost self-congratulatory confidence in our ability to quantify, measure and evaluate. And this love of measurement – which has spawned an impressive and sophisticated modern technology – has tended to enshrine our materialism. We like our 'realities' to be clearly identified, specific and objective: we are most comfortable when our existence divides into neat areas of activity and accomplishment, where we can be exactly sure and confident about what is going on.

The visionary perspective, however, reminds us that there are other dimensions of human existence which are less tangible than those we encounter in the material world. As we have already seen, we reflect these intangible qualities in our dreams, our fantasies and our imagination. Yet if we reflect on this, we must acknowledge that it is through the medium of human consciousness, and in turn the will, that our most deeply felt intuitions and inspirations can be given shape and form, becoming 'creations' in the physical world. Similarly, it is in our religious beliefs, our myths and cosmologies that we can find many neglected motifs of the inner realm – reminders of psychic energies which emanate from the visionary depths of the mind and spirit.

As children, many of us had parents who would read myths and legends to us, stimulating our love of the imaginal world, with its rich pageant of heroes and heroines, magical powers and mythical journeys. Yet later too, many of us learned to discard 'myths' as something innately 'untrue'. Indeed, the popular use of such words as 'myth' and 'fanciful' shows clearly that as a whole our culture does not especially value these facets of human experience. But have we, unintentionally perhaps, taken a wrong turn as a civilization? Have we ignored for too long the visionary aspects of human life and creativity?

Increasingly, researchers from within the ranks of the transpersonal and human potential movements, and those exploring the further reaches of parapsychology, are urging us to expand our perceptual frontiers, to look beyond the confines of reductionist materialism, and to develop new paradigms or frameworks which include the visionary perspective. When we look dispassionately at the world-view now emerging from these different areas of enquiry, there is good reason to consider quite different models of causality from those accepted by our mainstream, scientifically confined perspectives.

If one were to ask an Inuit (Eskimo) shaman for his world-view, for example, he would tell us that the universe is alive with gods and spirits. One such shaman told Danish explorer and anthropologist Knud Rasmussen that his food consisted 'entirely of souls'. For him the interconnectedness between the spirit world and the material world was abundantly obvious:

> All the creatures that we have to kill and eat, all those that we have to strike down and destroy to make clothes for ourselves, have souls, souls that do not perish with the body and which must therefore be pacified lest they should revenge themselves on us for taking away their bodies.[1]

Similarly, for the Jivaro of eastern Ecuador, as anthropologist Dr Michel Harner has noted:

> The normal waking life is explicitly viewed as 'false' or a 'lie' and it is firmly believed that truth about causality is to be found by entering the supernatural world, or what the Jivaro view as the 'real' world, for they feel that the events which take place within it underlie and are the basis for many of the surface manifestations and mysteries of daily life.[2]

And yet, while we might be inclined initially to dismiss the Inuit and Jivaro world-views out of hand as superstitious or irrational, we should also ask: are they perhaps pointing to dimensions of human awareness which we have chosen to ignore or devalue in our more 'advanced' culture? Certain areas of modern paranormal inquiry relate directly, and quite specifically, to this issue.

For much of its history the study of parapsychology has focused on such subjects as precognition, psychokinesis and telepathy, and has endeavoured to establish repeatable laboratory procedures to either validate or discredit the concepts of mind-to-mind communication or the possible influence of mind over matter, expressed for example in statistical analyses of the fall of dice or individual attempts to influence psychically the movement of small physical objects. From time to time such faddish phenomena as the psychic bending of knives and spoons (the so-called 'Geller effect') have also attracted public attention. However, it seems to me that parapsychological subject matter falls into two broad categories: purported skills and abilities said to occur beyond the realms of normal human functioning (for example, clairvoyant perceptions of the future, the ability to project psychic images onto camera film, move objects through mind-power alone, bend objects through ESP or engage in psychic surgery by causing incisions by 'psychic' means etc.), and phenomena which have implications for the human condition *per se*. The latter includes such subjects as out-of-the-body experiences (OBEs) and near-death experiences (NDEs), and incidents of hauntings, ghosts and apparitions – all of which pertain to the issue of the survival of human consciousness after death. This category of paranormal phenomena also perpetuates the perennial philosophical debate over dualism: is mind or consciousness a by-product of brain chemistry or, as the dualists maintain, a separate entity co-habiting with the brain while a person is alive (and therefore theoretically capable of surviving physical death)?

It is the second category of paranormal evidence I would like to consider here because there are clear implications from this area of inquiry for our concepts of human identity and the nature of life itself. And, as we will see later, taken as a whole, the sort of world-view which emerges from the OBE and NDE data, and the accumulated material on ghosts, mediums and hauntings, is strikingly similar to that of the classical shamanic viewpoint.

Out-of-the-Body Experiences (OBEs)

Out-of-the-body experiences have featured for many years in occult and Theosophical literature but only during the last twenty years or so has the phenomenon attracted serious scientific analysis and discussion. In recent times it has been the subject of detailed investigation by such researchers as Professor Charles Tart of the University of California at Davis, Dr Celia Green of the Institute of Psychophysical Studies at Oxford, noted parapsychologist D. Scott Rogo, Dr John Palmer of John F. Kennedy University, Orinda, California, and Dr Susan Blackmore of the University of Bristol, among many others.

An OBE is one where the person feels he is observing his surroundings from a position away from his body. Usually an OBE takes place during a state of drowsiness, relaxation, sickness or bodily inertness, although one of Celia Green's subjects suddenly felt himself floating high in the sky while riding a motorbike at speed through the countryside. Normally, however, the body is more passive.

Electroencephelograph (EEG) readings have revealed that OBEs share some characteristics with dreams although they do not coincide with rapid-eye-movement (REM) sleep. Also, they seem to be subject to *will*, unlike a dream, which incorporates random images, and they are characterized by a perceptive quality which often seems to the subject to be as clear and convincing as normal waking consciousness.

The three most noted modern pioneers of OBEs are Sylvan Muldoon, Oliver Fox (the pseudonym of Hugh Callaway) and more recently Robert A. Monroe, although other researchers like 'Yram' (Marcel Fohan), Ingo Swann and Blue Harary have also made significant contributions.

Sylvan Muldoon came from a family interested in spiritualist matters and it was while attending a Spiritualist meeting in Clinton, Iowa, at the age of twelve, that he had his first out-of-the-body venture. He felt that he had fallen into what he called a 'silent, dark and feelingless condition' and then suddenly found that he could project part of himself outside his body: 'I managed to turn around...There were two of me!'

Muldoon also describes a feature that for some time was regarded as characteristic of OBE projection: he noticed a silvery elastic cord joining his 'astral' body to his physical body.

As Muldoon 'walked around in the air' this cord maintained a connection between his astral consciousness and his inert slumbering body. He had simply transferred his perception outside his normal frame of reference. Muldoon came to believe that the astral body was in a sense 'more real' than the physical body, and in fact constituted the 'life' element. On death, Muldoon speculated, the astral body would sever the cord-link with the physical body and would not return. Russian parapsychologists have similarly formulated the idea of the 'bioplasmic body' – a type of energy prototype of the physical which, like the DNA code, regulates and maintains the physical organism.

Sylvan Muldoon, however, not only described his subsequent experiences in his important work *The Projection of the Astral Body* (1929), but went on to describe the means of achieving this state of consciousness. Anticipating some later experimenters, he evolved a technique of dream control whereby a person would try to will himself to dream a sequence of events which would involve the separation of the astral and physical bodies. One of these was to imagine oneself ascending in a lift and alighting on the top floor. Another was to swim, fly, or ride in a balloon.

Muldoon highlighted another aspect of the OBE. He found that usually the surroundings perceived in this state were similar to physical reality – an issue we will discuss further a little later on. An OBE projector might feel, for example, that he had travelled to a friend's or relative's house and was observing current, actual situations which could be verified for accuracy later on. However, at other times phantasy elements from the subconscious mind seem to intrude. These are found, for example in the OBE accounts of both Oliver Fox and Robert Monroe.

Oliver Fox's accounts of his OBEs first appeared in the *Occult Review* of 1920. Like Muldoon, there was a strong emphasis on dream control. Fox believed that the OBE occurred with the 'dream of knowledge', which took place when one *realized* that one was dreaming, and could then act purposefully within that framework. (This type of dream has more recently come to be known as the 'lucid dream'.) The dreamer could now enter a realm of consciousness which hitherto had been *unconscious*. He often found himself observing people shrouded in an aura of rich and dazzling colours, or sheathed in a type of energy field related to their emotional condition. Similar descriptions are given in Bishop Leadbeater's book on clairvoyance and the astral planes.

Initially Fox considered that the 'dream of knowledge' was the only means available for attaining the out-of-the-body state. Later he realized that relaxing the body could produce a similar effect. During such relaxation one would feel oneself overcome auto-hypnotically by a sense of numbness. Then it was almost like escaping through a trap-door in the brain. Fox called it the 'Pineal Door' method. On one occasion he felt that he was falling down a long shaft and, as Celia Green indicates, the tunnel is a common motif in OBEs. Fox was overcome with a sense of darkness and silence, and then noticed that he seemed to be naked and bleeding, as if from wounds. It occurred to him that he was dying. Then, as if he had suddenly entered the realm of Greek mythology, he heard a voice demanding: 'Say thou art Theseus. I am Oliver Fox.'

Strange mythological encounters and visions are commonly reported in the OBE state and lend credence to the view expressed in *The Tibetan Book of the Dead* that on death one's consciousness leaves the body and experiences visions of heavens and hells which are, in reality, states of harmony and disorder within the mind.

Robert Monroe first attracted international attention with the publication of his first book, *Journeys Out of the Body* in 1971. He published *Far Journeys* in 1985 and has a third volume, *The Ultimate Journey*, published in 1991.

Monroe studied engineering and journalism at Ohio State University and in 1939 went to New York, where he eventually created and produced some 400 radio and television network programmes over a period of twenty-one years. Later he formed his own production company and subsequently became a director and Vice-President of Mutual Broadcasting System Inc. – a position he held until 1956.

In the spring of 1958 Monroe had the first of what became a series of celebrated OBEs. He had been involved with experimentation into techniques of sleep-learning using a tape recorder, and believes that this may be linked to what happened to him.

One afternoon he was lying quietly on the couch in his living room when he felt a 'warm light' upon his body and began to 'vibrate' quite strongly. At the same time he found himself powerless to move and felt trapped, as if in a metal vice.

During the following months the same condition recurred several times. Monroe gradually discovered, however, that he could move his fingertips during the onset of 'vibrations' and found to his amazement that they were able to extend themselves and to 'feel' things beyond normal reach. It became apparent, though, that his fingers were not feeling in the physical sense, for they were able to penetrate through normally solid surfaces.

Shortly afterwards a similar experience occurred, except that Monroe now found himself extended and floating in his entirety, just below the surface of the ceiling of his room. Beneath him lay his immobile body on the bed. A sense of panic surged through his mind, for he suddenly seemed certain that he had died. In desperation he hurriedly sought to return to his body.

These fears proved groundless, and gradually he acquired more confidence. He subsequently began to explore the perceptual dimensions opened up by the use of his 'second body'. On several occasions Monroe would 'travel' to see his friends, noting in particular their conversation, their clothes and activities, so that on the next meeting he could confirm whether what he had 'seen' had in fact occurred. Once, during September 1958, he 'located' a friend outside his house when he had expected to see him sick in bed. Details of clothing and the exact time that his friend had unexpectedly left his house, were later confirmed as true.

Many of Monroe's OBEs were unusual in their clarity of detail but as he continued with his experimentation he soon began to encroach on other dimensions of the mind – realms that seemed more mythological, symbolic or surreal.

The ordinary realm of OBE consciousness Monroe called Locale I. It contained no strange beings, environments or places, and Monroe could sometimes verify his perceptions as physically valid, while they occurred 'at a distance' (This phenomenon is now known as 'remote viewing' in parapsychology.)

A quite different plane of events soon began to make its presence felt, however, and seemed to lead into broader and less tangible domains. Referring to this realm as Locale II, Monroe described it in *Journeys Out of the Body* as 'an immensity whose bounds are unknown, which has depth and dimension incomprehensible to the finite, conscious mind'. 'In this vastness,' he went on to say, 'lie all the aspects we attribute to heaven and hell.'

Monroe described Locale II as being populated by discarnate beings and the thought-forms of the living – a type of dream and phantasy dimension beyond the constrictions of time. 'Locale II,' wrote Monroe, 'is the *natural* environment of the Second Body.' Among the residents of Locale II were those who were 'alive but asleep, or drugged, or out of their Second Bodies, and quite probably those who are dead but still emotionally driven'. In this region too it was possible to meet 'all sorts of disjointed personalities and animate beings'.

It was Monroe's Locale II experiences which he regarded as most significant but it is worth digressing briefly to mention Monroe's third category, Locale III, which contained aspects not generally reported elsewhere in the literature of altered states of consciousness.

In this dimension a type of time-warp involving 'scientific inconsistencies' was experienced. People seemed to go about their business in much the same way as in Locale I, except that their technology was more bizarre – a surrealistic mirror-image of our own:

> Careful examination of one of the locomotives that pulled a string of old-fashioned looking cars showed it to be driven by a steam engine. The cars appeared to be made of wood, the locomotives of metal but of a different shape to our now obsolete types...

Despite the fact that this metal terrain was a phase out of step with normal reality, Monroe found himself projecting into its routines and environment. He seemed on one occasion to have assumed the 'body' of a married man within Locale III, in a process of 'reverse possession'.

Monroe's personal quest to explore altered states didn't stop with the publication of his first book however. Inundated with requests for further information, both from general readers and from academics and scientists, Monroe decided to establish a research laboratory to investigate OBEs more systematically.

The centre eventually became known as the Monroe Institute of Applied Sciences and is now located near Nellysford in Virginia's Blue Ridge Mountains. What is especially interesting is that Monroe's research demonstrated that certain frequencies of sound could induce OBEs quite naturally.

Monroe's original laboratory included three isolation booths connected independently to a central room both for physiological monitoring and to provide audio and electromagnetic signals to subjects in the booths. The booths themselves were totally dark and controlled for air, temperature and acoustics, and they allowed the subject to be monitored by eight-channel EEG (brain waves), EMG (muscle tone), pulse rate and body voltage equipment.

For several years the work was conducted on a voluntary basis with friends and a small group of participating scientists and doctors. The real breakthrough came in trying to keep the subjects from falling asleep. Monroe and his colleagues had the idea of using sound to guide the participants into that borderline state between sleep and fully conscious alertness. Certain sound patterns were discovered which enabled subjects to stay in the 'halfway' state for extended periods, and this led in turn to the discovery of sounds which were 'highly conducive' to OBEs and other altered states of consciousness. The latter sound system is now known as the Hemi-Sync process.

While most people in western cultures use the left side of the brain much more than the right, Monroe felt that it was important to use the potential of the right side as well. Hemi-Sync (short for 'hemispheric synchronization') uses frequencies of sound which help create simultaneously an identical waveform in both brain hemispheres.

When sounds of different wavelengths are played into opposite ears through stereo headphones, the brain assimilates the two pulses and 'hears' the difference between them. For example, if one were to feed 100 cycles per second (100 Hz) into one ear and 110 cycles per second (110 Hz) into the other, the difference would be a 10 Hz wave. This corresponds to a low alpha-wave frequency in the brain – a pattern which correlates with meditative states. Monroe's research programme is based on a comparable premise: that specific sound frequencies can be used to help people have OBEs. OBEs are sometimes associated with the theta wave frequency which ranges from 4 to 7 Hz, although other frequencies may be involved.

Monroe felt it would be good to develop an ongoing series of sessions for subjects to test and experience Hemi-Sync sound for themselves. It was in this way that what is now known as the Gateway Program came into existence. It began mostly by word of mouth but now several thousand subjects have explored it – including Dr Elisabeth Kubler-Ross. Many of the participants are 'pure right-brainers and mystics' according to Monroe, but the Program has also included scientists, psychologists and doctors from clinics and universities around the world. Monroe has also lectured at the Smithsonian Institute and his work has been presented to the American Psychiatric Association.

Not that Monroe's research is without controversy. His second book, *Far Journeys*, provides a log-book of different OBE projections and takes us into a world beyond the body where it is possible to communicate with discarnate and extra-terrestrial intelligence, experience fields of energy as if they were objectively real and travel in the mind's eye beyond the solar system. Monroe also feels it is possible to travel backwards and forwards in time: to access information from past history and to have apparently prophetic visionary insights into the future.

On the basis of his 'far journeys' Monroe now believes that there will be no nuclear war on a global scale, but that there will be astronomical contamination of some sort. He has also 'seen' a time when human beings will be able to limit their bodily dependence on food and, in time, eliminate it altogether. He also says that the world is surrounded by 'rings' of discarnate entities in varying states of evolution. All of us are immortal, he says, although some discarnate beings remain in an intermediate state, unaware that they are dead, while others appear to envelop themselves in 'emotionally based fears and drives which they attempt to act out but never conclude'. These beings are very much in need of psychic assistance to help them avoid remaining in a 'locked-in state' – a situation also reported by some psychic healers and spirit-channellers.

In an interview published in a Virginia newspaper, Monroe told a reporter:

Never mind religious beliefs...you're going to survive

physical death whether you like it or believe it or not. It's a fact. We've all been in other bodies in the past, and we will all be in other bodies in the future. Each consciousness is eternal, while bodies come and go...[3]

Explaining OBEs

Explanations for OBEs vary from researcher to researcher but as Dr Susan Blackmore has noted in her book *Beyond the Body*, they fall broadly into two categories: in one case it is assumed that some sort of energy body or 'consciousness' leaves the physical body and in the other that nothing leaves the body, and the experience is basically a component of hallucinatory, dream and memory elements.

Dr Blackmore herself takes the view that OBE travellers are projecting into a 'thought-created or mental world' and that this astral realm does not really coincide with the physical world, although at times it may appear to.

Also inclined towards the 'hallucinatory' interpretation of OBEs are researchers like Dr Ronald K. Siegel and Dr Jan Ehrenwald. Siegel, like Blackmore, believes that OBEs are simply ventures into mental space and do not coincide with physical reality, while Ehrenwald maintains that the OBE is a hallucination in which 'the experiencer proves immortality to himself by symbolically defying death'.

While the 'hallucinatory' explanation may on occasions be valid, and there is no doubt that some OBEs contain erroneous memory traces and blendings of actual and imaginary elements, such blanket dismissal does not appear to accord with the complete body of reported testimony. Hallucinations are by their nature fluid and unstable, while OBE subjects often report an essentially stable experience. And while Dr Blackmore favours an explanation which has OBE projectors 'jumping about in their cognitive maps, moving in every way their imagination allows', there are well-documented OBE accounts where other factors are involved. How are we to explain, for example, OBE accounts verified by a third party, or OBE projections involving a specific location that the subject had never in fact visited in real life? Also of interest, as reported by Dr Peter Bicknell (whose work is described below) is the fact that in those dissociative cases of projection where the OBE subject looks down upon a slumbering body, the person invariably sees an actual face image, not an inverted mirror-image which one would expect to see if the OBE was constructed purely from elements in the memory.

The so-called 'Wilmot Case', which took place in the late nineteenth century, was debated by such psychical researchers as Eleanor Sidgwick and F.W.H. Myers, and falls into the category of a purportedly 'objective' OBE. It is certainly difficult to dismiss as an 'hallucination':

> Mr S.R. Wilmot sailed from Liverpool to New York, passing through a severe storm. During the eighth night of the storm he had a dream in which he saw his wife come to the door of the stateroom. She looked about and seeing that her husband was not the only occupant of the room, hesitated a little, then advanced to his side, stooped down and kissed him, and after gently caressing him for a few moments, quietly withdrew.
>
> Upon awakening from his dream, Mr Wilmot was surprised to hear his fellow passenger, Mr William J. Tait say to him: 'You're a pretty fellow to have a lady come and visit you in this way.'
>
> Pressed for an explanation, Mr Tait related what he had seen while wide awake, lying in his berth. It exactly corresponded to the dream of Mr Wilmot!
>
> When meeting his wife in Watertown, Conn., Mr Wilmot was almost immediately asked by her: 'Did you receive a visit from me a week ago Tuesday?'
>
> Although Mr Wilmot had been more than a thousand miles at sea on that particular night, his wife asserted: '*It seemed to me that I visited you.*' She told her husband that on account of the severity of the weather and the reported loss of another vessel, she had been extremely anxious about him. On the night of the occurrence she had lain awake for a long time and about 4 o'clock in the morning it seemed to her that she left her physical self and went out to seek her husband, crossing the stormy sea until she came to his stateroom.
>
> She continued: 'A man was in the upper berth, *looking right at me*, and for a moment I was afraid to go in; but soon I went up to the side of your berth, bent down and kissed you, and embraced you, and then went away.[4]

Cases like this, and also that of 'G.V.' described below, tend towards the dualistic mind/body model rather than the hallucinatory hypothesis favoured by Blackmore, Siegel and Ehrenwald.

Dr Peter Bicknell of Monash University, Melbourne, has been actively collecting Australian OBE case histories in the same way that Celia Green has in Britain. To date he has assembled over 200 cases and has been able to analyse some of the common themes in the data. In 1975 Bicknell had an OBE himself. He was aware of dreaming and 'awoke' with a shock to find that his body was paralysed. There were jarring effects in his body and they seemed to reach a crescendo in his head, where all sensation was for the most part focused. He perceived a duplicate body rising from his bed at an angle but his head was not yet fully dissociated. Bicknell became frightened and panicked, then suddenly found himself back in his body with a thump - a very common reaction, as international surveys of OBEs have shown.

Dr Bicknell's findings on OBEs have complemented those of Celia Green, Scott Rogo and other international researchers. Most people, according to Bicknell, find that the will is the means of directing an OBE and that the common sensation is one of conscious awareness outside the body and almost total independence. Most people see in colour, others in sepia or grey, and occasionally subjects report 360° vision and tactile awareness. At the time Muldoon and Fox were writing it used to be common to talk of an astral double connected to the physical body by an umbilical cord, but in Celia Green's study, only 3.5 per cent reported seeing a cord. Peter Bicknell's study turned up only two people out of 200 who reported this. Some subjects entered a sphere or 'balloon of light' when they projected and one person felt the wind around her, even though she could not directly perceive a duplicate body. Bicknell feels this may be rather like the 'phantom limb effect' experienced by people who have had a limb amputated and yet retain the sensation of full effectiveness.

One of the most interesting cases in the Bicknell survey involved a young woman, known in the survey as 'G.V.', who wished to apply for a position at the health centre in Queenscliff, a town located on the Victorian coast not far from Geelong. She had never visited the town and was thinking about it as she went to sleep one evening, only to discover that she had brought about an OBE by dwelling on it. In her projected state she found herself hovering at tree-top height above a road which was signposted as leading to Queenscliff; it was apparently a moonlit night but she perceived the whole environment in sepia and not in colour. She followed the road into the town, noting unusual mud-flats beside the road and finally details of Queenscliff's main street. One building decorated with iron tracery she took to be a hotel and later she noticed on the cliff-edge beyond the beach a tower which might have been a lighthouse but which was not clearly visible. Later she willed herself to visit the health centre and her vision focused on a square building with pale bricks, wide doors and large, curtained windows. Before she could enter the building she blacked out and returned to her body in bed.

Dr Bicknell decided to check this case out in full and drove to Queenscliff to verify the account. The mud-flats were clearly visible beside the road and the most conspicuous building in the main street featured elaborate wrought-iron work. However, it was not a hotel but a local government office. On a cliff in the distance was a lighthouse but there was also a very obvious pier on the beachfront which 'G.V.' had not alluded to. Bicknell then went to check the health centre which, as 'G.V.' had indicated, was indeed square in plan, was constructed of pale bricks and had curtained windows and wide doors. However there was also a piece of walling in front of the building bearing the full name of the health centre which 'G.V.' had apparently not noticed during her OBE. Bicknell returned to Melbourne and contacted 'G.V.', who stuck to her account and signed a sworn affidavit that she had not as yet visited the town physically. Puzzled by the two main omissions in her OBE account – the pier and the health centre inscription – Bicknell decided to return to Queenscliff at night. He found that the centre was unlit and that the identifying name would have been hard to see from certain vantage points, and also that the pier appeared to blend with its surroundings, making it hard to pick out clearly. However he also noted that the lighthouse would have been emitting flashing lights periodically, which 'G.V.' apparently did not see. His conclusion about the case was that his subject appeared to enter a domain in the OBE state which was at least in part identical to the real, physical world but was not totally the same. And yet there seemed to be sufficient detailed recall not to identify the experience as a hallucination or dream.

As a result of his survey, Dr Bicknell favours the 'dual

consciousness' concept in accounting for OBEs: in other words, people who project really do perceive the world from their new vantage point. In his survey he has found that 81 per cent observe their physical bodies during the OBE and several subjects have been surprised by seeing themselves 'as others might see them' – that is, not in the mirror-image with which each of us tends to identify. Since when we dream about ourselves the content programmed into the dream from our waking consciousness is invariably mirror-reversed, Dr Bicknell feels that OBEs are definitely in a category different from dreams and hallucinations.[5]

Near-Death Experiences (NDEs)

The term 'near-death experience' is a recent one – it was coined in 1975 by the American philosopher and teacher, Dr Raymond Moody – but like the out-of-the-body experience the phenomenon is probably a universal human occurrence. Shamanism, the most ancient religious tradition of all, deals essentially with the spiritual flight of the soul to different cosmic realms and in pre-literate societies the shaman has often been referred to as a 'master of death'. Similarly in the *Dialogues* of the sixth-century Pope, Gregory the Great, we find an interesting account of a soldier's return from apparent death:

> A certain soldier in this city of ours [Rome] happened to be struck down. He was drawn out of his body and lay lifeless, but he soon returned [to life] and described what befell him. At that time there were many people experiencing these things. He said that there was a bridge, under which ran a black, gloomy river which breathed forth an intolerably foul-smelling vapour. But across the bridge there were delightful meadows carpeted with green grass and sweet-smelling flowers. The meadows seemed to be meeting places for people clothed in white...[6]

According to Gregory's description the soldier observed a type of spiritual struggle during his NDE: a pilgrim crossing the bridge had to fend off hideous evil spirits who were trying to drag him into the vile, hellish river, while other 'good spirits' were endeavouring to assist in his salvation. Unfortunately the soldier did not learn the final outcome of this struggle for he returned to his body, and to waking consciousness, before the conflict was resolved.

In our own time, however, the NDE has not usually been couched in terms of a cosmic struggle and NDEs featuring hell-like imagery are quite rare. Indeed, the NDE seems not to depend on one's personal commitment to any theological doctrine or concept of an afterlife, nor does it usually involve a tangible polarity between good and evil. In fact, during the last decade a number of transpersonal researchers and parapsychologists have greatly assisted in 'de-mythologizing' the NDE.

We usually define death as the absence of all visible signs of life – there is no heartbeat or respiration and brain-wave activity has apparently ceased (that is, any EEG monitoring of electrical brain impulses would register as zero). To all intents and purposes such a person is clinically dead. The NDE, by definition, involves the return from apparent clinical death to waking consciousness and is in itself a phenomenon that has been greatly assisted by advances in medical technology. It is only because the techniques of medical resuscitation and life-support are now so sophisticated that we have a burgeoning literature which describes the accounts of people who have seemingly 'died' and yet lived to tell the tale. Those accounts, and the scientific and medical commentaries accompanying them, provide a new focus for the philosophical issue of mind and body in the debate over consciousness and 'soul'.

Among the first modern accounts anticipating the NDE studies was the work of Swiss geologist Professor Albert Heim, who collected data on the experiences of people who had nearly died in mountain-climbing accidents or in warfare. Heim's writings were translated in the 1970s by Russell Noyes and Ray Kletti, and included instances where people faced with the prospect of imminent death experienced a panoramic life-review or heard transcendental music.

Also preceding the more recent NDE literature were the findings of Dr Karlis Osis, a Latvian-born parapsychologist based in New York, who conducted a scientific survey of death-bed visionary experiences. Osis despatched questionnaires to 10,000 physicians and nurses and received 540 responses. On the basis of these he published a book entitled *Death-bed Observations by Physicians and Nurses* in 1961. In this book Osis noted that terminal subjects often experienced periods of bliss and spiritual peace prior to death. Some also saw apparitions of deceased relatives or friends coming to greet them, and seemed to realize intuitively that these figures were about to help them through the transition of death itself.

The first widespread popular awareness of the NDE phenomenon came, however, with the publication of Dr Raymond Moody's *Life After Life* in 1975. Moody had begun collecting anecdotal accounts of near-death incidents in 1972 and his book was based on 150 accounts from people who contacted him as a result of articles he had written or lectures he had given on this topic. Moody gives this characteristic description of a typical NDE:

> A man is dying, and as he reaches the point of greatest physical distress, he hears himself pronounced dead by his doctor. He begins to hear an uncomfortable noise, a loud ringing or buzzing, and at the same time feels himself moving very rapidly through a long dark tunnel. After this, he suddenly finds himself outside of his own physical body, but still in the immediate physical environment, and he sees his own body from a distance, as though he is a spectator. He watches the resuscitation attempt from this unusual vantage point and is in a state of emotional upheaval.
>
> After a while, he collects himself and becomes more accustomed to his odd condition. He notices that he still has a 'body', but one of a very different nature and with very different powers from the physical body he has left behind. Soon other things begin to happen. Others come to meet and to help him. He glimpses the spirits of relatives and friends who have already died, and a loving, warm spirit of a kind he has never encountered before - a being of light - appears before him. This being asks him a question, non-verbally, to make him evaluate his life and helps him along by showing him a panoramic, instantaneous playback of the major events of his life. At some point he finds himself approaching some sort of barrier or border, apparently representing the limit between earthly life and the next life. Yet he finds that he must go back to the earth, that the time for his death has not yet come. At this point he resists, for by now he is taken up with his experiences in the afterlife and does not want to return. He is overwhelmed by intense feelings of joy, love and peace. Despite his attitude, though, he somehow reunites with his physical body and lives.

> Later he tries to tell others, but he has trouble doing so. In the first place, he can find no human words adequate to describe these unearthly episodes. He also finds that others scoff, so he stops telling other people. Still, the experience affects his life profoundly, especially his views about death and its relationship to life.[7]

Moody's book became a catalyst and inspiration to others interested in this field and there have since been more systematic research studies of the phenomenon. Among those who have greatly assisted in this work are Dr Kenneth Ring, Professor of Psychology at the University of Connecticut, his British colleague Dr Margot Grey, founder of the International Association for Near-Death Studies (IANDS) in the United Kingdom, world-famous thanatologist Dr Elisabeth Kubler-Ross, and cardiologist Dr Michael Sabom of Emory University, Atlanta.

Kenneth Ring's *Life at Death*, published in 1980, was the first scientific study of NDEs and was based on over 100 interviews with subjects who had survived near-death. Ring followed it in 1984 with *Heading Toward Omega*, a lucid overview of the implications of the NDE and its capacity for triggering self-transformation and spiritual awakening. Ring and Grey have both described the 'core' NDE in broadly the same way: an altered state of feeling (peace, joy, serenity etc.); a sense of movement or separation from the body (an aerial view of the body, generally heightened awareness); a journey through a tunnel towards either a transcendent dimension or some other, more tangible realm (a celestial valley, garden or city), the experience of light and beauty; encounters in the spirit world with deceased relatives, spirits or 'guides' and sometimes religious figures like Jesus or 'God'. They have also sought to evaluate the impact such visionary experiences have had on the lives of the NDE subjects themselves.

Both Ring and Grey came to the conclusion that the 'core' NDE was largely 'invariant', occurring in much the same form (though not with all the characteristics necessarily present in every individual case), irrespective of nationality, social class, age, sex, educational level or occupation. What is highly significant about this finding is that the core aspects of the NDE are comparatively constant irrespective of whether that person is a religious believer, atheist or agnostic: in other words, the NDE seems to be pointing towards characteristics of universal human consciousness rather than towards a wide variety of disjointed or divergent sensory experiences such as one might expect if the experience was purely hallucinatory. To this extent the NDE seems to be telling us about the process of dying itself and the various stages or transitions of human consciousness which might occur beyond bodily death.

Once again we have the difficult issue of body, mind and spirit to resolve: during an NDE, is the subject projecting consciousness beyond the physical body and, if so, how is such a thing possible?

In Kenneth Ring's *Life at Death* survey: '97.4 per cent of core experiencers felt that their bodies were light or absent; 94.6 per cent found their sense of time either expanded or absent, and 81.8 per cent experienced space as either extended, infinite or absent.' As Ring noted: 'For most respondents, body, time and space simply disappear – or, to put it another way, they are no longer meaningful constructs.'[8]

Such aspects of the NDE, as one would expect, have proved problematic for reductionist researchers keen on explaining away the phenomenon as illusory or hallucinatory. For to admit the possibility of consciousness beyond the physical organism would entail the total reformulation of currently held frameworks of human perception and 'consciousness'.

Among the most commonly reported 'explanations' from this camp are that NDEs are delusory experiences which result from temporal lobe seizure or loss of oxygen as one approaches death; that they are simply re-enactments of the birth process; that they are caused by anaesthetic drugs; and that they are the symptoms of psychological factors related to the likely onset of death.

In fairness to these viewpoints it might be worthwhile summarizing the shortcomings of these explanations before discussing in more detail some of the key areas of the NDE and its implications.

Hallucinations and delusions: Dr Michael Sabom was particularly impressed in his medical survey by the ability of some autoscopic (out-of-the-body/self-observing) NDE subjects to report details of actual events (medical equipment, surgical procedures, real conversations) from a detached and elevated position. 'The details of these perceptions were found to be accurate in all instances where corroborating evidence was available.' Sabom also reported that some NDE subjects also experienced hallucinations during their coma states and were able to distinguish clearly between the two categories of perception.[9]

Temporal lobe seizure: Seizures deriving from the temporal lobes (or non-motor portions) of the brain involve sensory distortions of the size or location of objects close by, and sometimes a feeling of detachment from the environment. They are also characterized by feelings of fear and loneliness and visual or auditory hallucinations. On the other hand, many NDE subjects report accurate, undistorted perceptual fields and may feel elated or relaxed about their dissociated condition.

Loss of oxygen in the brain: Under normal circumstances, if the oxygen supply to the brain is reduced, this produces in turn a state of mental confusion and cognitive dysfunction. This is certainly not characteristic of the NDE, which is often described by subjects as profoundly real and perceptually coherent. Some subjects suffering from brain hypoxia (oxygen loss) – for example, mountain climbers who have trekked in rarefied atmospheres – find they experience an onset of laziness and irritability, and they may also find it difficult to remember what they were thinking or doing at the time. Many NDE subjects, on the other hand, are so awed by the clarity and detail of their experiences that they remember them for many years afterwards (see the Allan Lewis case summarized below).

Reliving the birth process: If NDEs, which are characterized by feelings of passing through a tunnel towards light, are somehow the result of the normal birth process, then people born by Caesarean section should not have them. Dr Susan Blackmore gave a questionnaire to 254 people, of whom 36 had been born by Caesarean. 'Both groups reported the same proportion of out-of-the-body and tunnel experiences,' she has written. 'It could be that the experiences are based on the *idea* of birth in general, but this drastically weakens the theory.'[10]

Anaesthetic drugs: There are several cases of NDE subjects who received no anaesthetic drugs during their hospitalization, so this explanation, if indeed it is one at all, would not apply in many instances. While it is true that some dissociative anaesthetics like ketamine hydrochloride (Ketalar) may produce an experience in which one's consciousness appears distinct from the body and there may also be an awareness of journeying through tunnels in space, Ketalar is not widely used in human medical treatment and is now for the most part restricted to veterinary practice. In general, drug-induced hallucinations seem to be markedly different from NDEs. Dr Sabom notes that drug experiences are 'highly variable and idiosyncratic' and 'markedly different from NDEs, which always show a remarkable degree of invariance'.

Psychological factors: One psychological view of NDEs is that the experience derives from 'depersonalization'. This theory, advanced by Noyes and Kletti (who translated the Heim material) argues that the ego has to protect itself from impending death and thus creates a perceptual scenario which supports the feeling of continuing mental integration. As Dr Noyes has said: 'As an adaptive pattern of the nervous system it alerts the organism to its threatening environment while holding potentially disorganising emotion in check.' Dr Sabom rejects this view as a blanket explanation of the NDE because there were subjects in his survey who had out-of-the-body NDEs without being aware psychologically of any likelihood of imminent death. Some of these were subjects who experienced loss of waking consciousness without warning, due to a stoppage of the heart. Also, as Dr Margot Grey has indicated, 'depersonalization' is unable to account for NDE subjects who have claimed to have had meetings with relatives who had recently died but whom the NDE subject *did not know* had died. (Here the NDE subject would learn of the relative's actual death only after recovering from the NDE: the expectation prior to the NDE would be that the person was still alive.)

It may be worthwhile at this point to quote a few brief examples of what NDE subjects actually report, because their testimonies are our starting point and they provide insights into the *processes* that seem to be involved:

> I felt as though I was looking down at myself, as though I was way out here in space...I felt sort of separated.

> It was a wonderful feeling. It was marvellous. I felt very light and didn't know where I was...And then I thought that something was happening to me. This wasn't night. I wasn't dreaming...And then I felt a wonderful feeling as if I was out in space.

> I felt myself being separated: my soul drawing apart from the physical being, was drawn upward seemingly to leave the earth and to go upward where it reached a greater Spirit with whom there was a communion, producing a remarkable new relaxation and deep security.

There is also the remarkable case reported by Kimberly Clark – a social worker at Harborview Medical Center in Seattle – which, as with the above, clearly indicates a dualistic model of mind and body.

Ms Clark's subject was a migrant worker named Maria who had suffered a coronary attack while visiting Seattle. She was resuscitated and interviewed later the same day. Maria told Kimberly Clark that she had had an NDE in which she floated to the ceiling and watched the doctors below. She could hear the conversations taking place during surgery but then became distracted and found herself floating outside the hospital building and above the emergency room driveway. She then seemed to be level with a third-floor ledge, where she spotted a tennis shoe that had been left there. Maria urged Kimberly Clark, who was highly dubious about the whole incident, to go and see whether the shoe was in fact there. Clark decided to humour her.

> With mixed emotions I went outside and looked up at the ledge but could not see much at all. I went up to the third floor and began going in and out of patients' rooms and looking out of their windows, which were so narrow that I had to press my face to the screen just to see the ledge at all. Finally I found a room where I pressed my face to the glass and looked down and saw the tennis shoe! My vantage point was very different from what Maria's had to have been for her to notice that the little toe had worn a place in the shoe and that the lace was stuck under the heel and other details about the side of the shoe not visible to me. The only way she would have had such a perspective was if she had been

floating right outside and at very close range to the tennis shoe. I retrieved the shoe and brought it back to Maria; it was very concrete evidence for me.[11]

Spirits of the Dead in NDEs

It is not uncommon for NDE subjects to report contact with deceased relatives or friends, or even with 'God' or 'Jesus'. In Dr Sabom's survey of 116 NDE subjects, 28 described encounters with other personages. One of Dr Sabom's case studies involved a seriously injured soldier, and his account of his deceased colleagues is intriguingly matter-of-fact:

> I came out of my body, and perceived me laying on the ground with three limbs gone...What makes this so real was that the thirteen guys that had been killed the day before that I had put in plastic bags were right there with me. And more than that, during the course of that month of May, my regular company lost forty-two dead. All forty-two of those guys were there. They were not in the form we perceive the human body, and I can't tell you what form they were in because I don't know. But I know they were there. I felt their presence. We communicated without talking with our voices. There was no sympathy, no sorrow. They were already where they were. They didn't want to go back. That was the basic tone of our communication...that we were all happy right where we were.[12]

Another account of contact with a discarnate intelligence coupled with clear dissociation from the body is mentioned in W.O. Stevens' book *The Mystery of Dreams*, published in 1950. Here Stevens describes the case of Iris Yeoman, who had suffered from a strong fear of death. This reached a type of climax when she was eighteen years old. One night while she was resting in her bed, she felt herself to be dying, even though she was in good health at the time. She suddenly saw several deceased relatives by her bedside and experienced the classical release of the 'spirit' from the body:

> A curious sensation began at my feet. Almost like a tight glove being pulled from a finger. This pulling sensation travelled up my body until it reached my shoulders, and

throat. Then came a second of blank unconsciousness, and I found myself standing beside the bed looking down at the body on the bed. Had I actually lived inside that? To my surprise I found that I still had hands, and feet, and a body, for I had always regarded the soul as something without shape and void. In those days I had read no Spiritualistic books on after-death conditions, and to find that though I was 'dead' I still had form, was new to me. I looked with pity, not unmixed with contempt, at those who were mourning me. Then suddenly, on the blank wall on the side of the room farthest from the door, appeared an opening, like a tunnel, and at the far end a light. The power that had drawn my body from me, drew me irresistibly towards this passageway, which as I moved nearer to it seemed to lead steeply upwards. Without any exertion on my part, I was drawn up the passage and soon found myself standing at the top, on the summit of a hill covered with the greenest grass I had ever seen. I glanced round. The country was undulating and beautiful. Woodland scenery gave way to the glint of water, here and there. There was no sun visible, but the light had a wonderful and unusual quality.

Beside me I found a very tall veiled figure. I could not see the face, but I knew that he was a trusted friend. I knew, too, that he was smiling at me, when he spoke. 'Look back at the way you have come,' he said. I looked down the passage. My body still lay upon the bed. My friends were still grieving for me. Then I was told to shift my attention and immediately I found that I could see the entire world as clearly as I had observed the details of my room. The earth was shrouded in clouds of depression, fear and pain, my heart swelled with pity. I held out my arms and cried to my friends, and to the world: 'Look up. Look up. Can't you see that I am alive, and well, and happy? Far more alive than I ever was on earth. There is no death. Death is life. Then I woke, and the old terror had passed for ever.[13]

Other accounts of spirits encountered in NDEs take us even further into metaphysical territory. One of these is provided by Dr George Ritchie, a practising psychiatrist and author of *Return From Tomorrow*. Ritchie nearly died from pneumonia while serving in the military towards the end of World War

Two and had an NDE. It was a meeting with Ritchie which first stimulated Dr Raymond Moody's interest in NDEs.

Ritchie was pronounced clinically dead for a period of nine minutes and during this NDE had an experience in his astral form which took him into a bar. All of the patrons physically present had an 'aura' but there were other non-physical beings like himself, and some of these were trying to pick up glasses in order to have a drink. In this endeavour they were unsuccessful: 'Their hands just passed straight through the tumblers. It was obvious that none of the patrons could see or feel these thirsty, disembodied beings.'

The bar itself was a popular drinking place for sailors on service leave. Dr Ritchie continues:

> One very intoxicated sailor rose unsteadily from his stool and then fell heavily to the floor, unconscious. I was staring in amazement as the bright cocoon around him simply opened up. It parted at the crown of his head and began peeling away. Instantly, quicker than I'd ever seen anyone move, one of the insubstantial beings who had been standing at the bar was on top of him. In the next instant, to my mystification, the springing figure had vanished. It all happened even before the two men beside him had dragged the unconscious body from under their feet. One minute I'd distinctly seen two beings like myself, yet, by the time they'd propped the sailor up against the wall there was only one.

Ritchie watched this happen again, twice, and went on to comment:

> Presumably these substanceless creatures once had solid bodies as I myself had. Suppose that when they had been in these bodies they had developed dependence on alcohol that went beyond the physical. That became mental. Spiritual even. Then when they lost that body, except when they briefly could take possession of another one, they would be cut off for all eternity from the thing they could never stop craving.[14]

Ritchie's NDE account provides a fascinating insight into the 'astral' mechanism behind some 'possession' cases and also reveals a plane of existence – accessed only in an altered state of consciousness like an NDE – where discarnate beings endeavour to interact with the living.

Another example of this phenomenon, though quite different in content, is provided by the remarkable case of Allan Lewis, who now works as an industrial chemist in the Australian state of Victoria. Lewis had contracted scarlet fever when he was two years old and this resulted in a rheumatic heart condition. In April 1946, while he was a student at Devonport High School in Tasmania, he experienced three heart attacks in a single day. His account, first broadcast as part of an ABC Radio programme entitled 'And When I Die, Will I Be Dead?' is, in my view, one of the most extraordinary reports in the entire NDE literature. Lewis' account, which is quite lengthy and has recently been published in book form, includes all the characteristic OBE/NDE perceptions, some of them purely physical in orientation, others possibly more symbolic or metaphorical.[15]

During the first of his three NDEs, Lewis was clearly able to see his teachers as they endeavoured to revive his body: here he was in a classically autoscopic position above his body. As with Ritchie's discarnate beings, Lewis tried to interact.

> They were doing their best to do something for me. I moved down to Miss Brown who was massaging my legs and tried to get her to stop because I knew then that I was dead. I said to her 'I'm dead. Don't bother with me, Miss Brown' and she took no notice of me. So I tried to grab hold of her arm to move her and my hand went straight through her arm. I just couldn't get a grip on her.

Later Lewis moved outside the school building in spirit form to a playgroup where some girls were playing hockey. Here he observed the spirit of an old lady trying to make contact with one of the players.

> I can remember approaching this old lady spirit and saying, 'It's no good, you can't get in touch with them'...There were quite a few other spirit beings around. I could see them. I didn't try to contact them. They all seemed to be doing something and moving about and not taking any notice of me. I went back to my body at this stage and I don't know by what mechanism but I got back into my body.

Lewis revived from his first NDE and was able to converse with his teachers. He was then examined by a local doctor, Dr Addison, who began to place a stethoscope on his chest. However, at this stage Lewis felt another heart attack coming on. He says that once again he left his body and was able to hear the headmaster lament: 'I think we've lost him...' Again he found himself outside the school buildings, where he was able to wander through the nearby streets in his astral form.

> Then I saw a lot of other spirits. I saw some of them moving through trees. Most of them were moving at about six feet above the ground and they seemed to be quite human in shape. Some were grey and some were quite brightish. They seemed to be clothed. They definitely didn't have wings like the typical image of angels. They seemed to have four limbs and a head. Then I decided to come back to my body to see what was going on there. The doctor was still thumping away at my chest and I went back into my body and the pain came back.

Once again Lewis was able to speak to the headmaster, and to Dr Addison who told him that he had a rheumatic heart condition and advised that he should recuperate at home for a few weeks and avoid playing sport until his condition improved. Meanwhile Lewis lay down to rest and a senior mistress placed a blanket over him to keep him warm.

However, after about another forty minutes, he was alarmed to feel a much more painful attack building up. For a time the pain was overwhelmingly intense – 'I wanted to do something that would kill me and ease my condition' – but then the pain subsided 'and a beautiful feeling of peace came over me'. Lewis now found himself once again outside his body and assumed that he had finally died. As before, he noticed a number of human spirits and conversed with them. One was a woman who urged him to return to his body, but another was that of a school teacher, Colin Wright, who had been at Lewis' school but had died in a training accident in Kenya in 1942. Wright had brought with him another person called Lucas, 'dressed in ancient clothing', who could apparently help Lewis with his heart condition.

While Lucas was attending to Lewis' heart, Wright also drew Lewis' attention to some 'grey and drab' spirit figures who he said were suicide victims. They seemed to be wandering aimlessly in a limbo condition, and Wright cautioned Lewis that he must never again consider the possibility of suicide.

Lewis reports that he now felt as if he were descending into a bottomless well and moving at incredible speed. He passed into a luminescent domain where details of a shimmering 'ivory' city came into view. Here he encountered a distantly related aunt and also the spirit form of a young boy, Eric Wilmott, who had drowned in a river near his school four years earlier. They discussed details of the incident, and the ensuing peace which followed the trauma of dying, and later Lewis was able to discuss the matter with Wilmott's older brother, who was amazed by Lewis' description since most of this information had been known only to members of Wilmott's family. Lewis says that later in this NDE he also met a number of other relatives of his own 'who died before I was born. I didn't know them, but I was introduced to them and we began talking.'

Lewis' third NDE also included an amazing meeting with an entity he refers to as 'The Light', although this being seems not to have been 'Jesus' or 'God'. The Light provided him with some playback details of events in his life so far, enabling him to be his own judge, and then offered him the opportunity to visit a large building which seemed to be 'alive' with electrical impulses. Here Lewis seemed to be bombarded with information: 'I was picking up the entire history of the human race.'

Soon afterwards Lewis was once again aware of Eric Wilmott, who asked him if he was happy to return to the physical world. Lewis said he was worried about once again journeying through the well but Wilmott reassured him: 'You just walk out of here. Just go straight through the wall. It's like stepping out of a bubble. You'll be above your body...' Then he added: 'Don't forget to breathe when you get back to your body. You must breathe.'

Lewis says that at this stage he apparently returned to his body and was able to start breathing, although the pain also returned at this time.

During the ensuing weeks Lewis tried to talk to both his scoutmaster and a church minister about the subject of death but neither were interested in such a topic and they didn't wish to pursue it. So Lewis kept his experiences to himself until he saw a television interview with Dr Elisabeth Kubler-Ross many years later. When Lewis told his wife that he had had similar NDEs as a schoolboy she was 'quite unbelieving' and it was not until the radio programme was compiled - some thirty-two years after the incident and yet still with extraordinary clarity of detail - that Lewis' account was able to be related in full.

Lewis continues to live what he describes as a comparatively ordinary suburban existence but was greatly relieved to learn, via the Kubler-Ross programme, that other people had had experiences like his. It is also interesting to note that when Lewis visited two different heart specialists at the age of twenty-six, he was told that his heart was now in good condition. Lewis says that his NDEs have not dramatically changed his life but that he is no longer afraid of death: 'Death is nothing to be feared. The only bad thing about death is the grief that it leaves behind. The people that stay - they are people that suffer, not the person that dies.'

Lewis' case represents the further end of the spectrum in NDEs and is fascinating because after moving from a mostly physically oriented locale (the school-room, teachers, and audible conversation) it provides points of overlap with the spirit world, before becoming more mystical in orientation. Even so, the different conversations with Eric Wilmott - later discussed with Wilmott's brother in real life - add a pragmatic dimension to what would otherwise be regarded as a substantially 'symbolic' or 'metaphorical' sequence.

Incidents like the Allan Lewis NDEs provide a distinct challenge to the reductionist hypotheses summarized above and yet they also require a somewhat sophisticated interpretation. If we compare the NDE account with the writings of OBE subjects like Robert Monroe and Oliver Fox, it seems possible that there is some kind of continuum between physical perceptions in this state and mythic or symbolic ones, and that the latter may be heightened in intensity during an NDE.

This type of perspective is also supported by the well-known parapsychologist D. Scott Rogo who, in his recently published book *The Return from Silence*, suggests that the NDE is really a type of OBE but the visionary aspects of the NDE 'point to a greater spiritual reality'. Rogo believes that the visionary components of the experience only arise when a genuine OBE is taking place and what he calls the 'eschatological' NDE is 'not merely a transformative psychological experience but a deeply spiritual encounter with some sort of Ultimate Reality – a reality buried deeply behind the NDE's metaphoric language'.[16]

Apparitions, Ghosts and Hauntings

The literature on this subject is vast and owes much of its impetus to the pioneering efforts of the Society for Psychical Research (SPR), first established in England in 1882 by Frederic Myers, Henry Sidgwick and Edmund Gurney. The search for an all-encompassing explanation for ghosts, apparitions and the manifestations of psychic mediumism attracted such distinguished physicists as Sir William Crookes, Sir Oliver Lodge and Sir William Barrett to the Society, and Carl Jung, Sigmund Freud and the noted physiologist Charles Richet were also members. Today, however, the task is not so much the continuing accumulation of data and case studies – vast amounts already exist – but the development of a theory or model which accounts for different aspects of such paranormal phenomena and which is able to relate it to the study of 'consciousness' or 'the soul'.

In his classical study, *Apparitions*, first published in 1953, G.N.M. Tyrrell proposed that apparitions be divided into four classes: ghosts or haunting apparitions, crisis apparitions, post-mortem cases and experimental cases. This type of classification has been retained in more recent parapsychological works like Professor Arthur Ellison's *The Reality of the Paranormal* and will also provide the basis of the material summarized here.

It is worth noting initially, though, that apparitions can be of both the living and the dead, and this is clearly relevant if we are considering the hypothesis (supported, I would suggest, by much of the OBE and NDE data) that in certain circumstances it is possible to project consciousness beyond the body. However, we will consider such implications later. The popular notion of apparitions, ghosts and hauntings, however, is very much linked to the subject of death, post-mortem survival and the realm of the 'spirits'.

Haunting Apparitions

One of the most famous cases in the SPR archives is that of the so-called 'Cheltenham Hauntings'. The distinguished parapsychologist Professor Robert H. Thouless regarded this case as 'the best study of an apparitional haunting' and even sceptical researchers have been cautious in dismissing it, since the apparition was seen at different times by at least seventeen different people and heard by as many as twenty, over a period of possibly eighty years. The location of the hauntings was a house that still stands in the corner of Pittville Circus Road and All Saints Road, Cheltenham, England. Its residents were the Despard family – Captain F.W. Despard, his wife and six children – and the apparition was of a tall, weeping woman dressed in black who invariably appeared holding a handkerchief near her face. The first sightings occurred in 1882 and Frederic Myers interviewed the family and house staff two years later, while the sightings were still continuing. There was a remarkable uniformity in the reports of all witnesses, even when there had been no contact between them.

Rosina Despard first saw the apparition in June 1882.

> I had gone up to my room, but was not yet in bed, when I heard someone at the door, and went to it, thinking that it might be my mother. On opening the door, I saw no-one; but on going a few steps along the passage, I saw the figure of a tall lady, dressed in black, standing at the head of the stairs. After a few momemts she descended the stairs, and I followed for a short distance, feeling curious what it could be. I had only a small piece of candle, and it suddenly burnt itself out; and being unable to see more, I went back to my room.
>
> The figure was that of a tall lady, dressed in black soft woollen material, judging from the slight sound in moving. This is all I noticed then; but on further occasions, when I was able to observe her more closely, I saw the upper part of the left side of her forehead, and a little more of her hair above. Her left hand was nearly hidden by her sleeve and a fold of her dress. As she held it down a portion of a widow's cuff was visible on both wrists, so that the whole impression was that of a lady in widow's weeds. There was no cap on the head but a general effect of blackness suggests a bonnet, with long veil or a hood.[17]

Rosina Despard saw the figure six times between 1882 and 1884 and then, also in 1882, Rosina's sister, Mrs Kinloch – who was visiting the family at the time – saw the figure cross the hall and pass into the drawing room. Because of the dark clothing, Mrs Kinloch assumed that the person she had seen was a Sister of Mercy but she was told there was no such visitor in the house. When a servant went to look in the drawing room she found it empty.

In January 1884 Rosina Despard again saw the apparition and this time tried to speak to it.

> I opened the drawing-room door softly and went in, standing just by it. She came in past me and walked up to the sofa and stood still there, so I went up to her and asked her if I could help her. She moved, and I thought she was going to speak, but she gave only a slight gasp and moved towards the door. Just by the door I spoke to her again, but she seemed as if she were quite unable to speak. She walked into the hall, then by the side door she seemed to disappear as before.[18]

One evening in July 1884 Rosina again saw the ghostly figure in the drawing room. Her father and sisters were sitting with her but Rosina was 'astonished' that no one else in the room seemed able to see the phantom image.

> She was so very distinct to me. My youngest brother, who had before seen her, was not in the room. She stood behind the couch for about half an hour, and then as usual walked to the door. I went after her, on the excuse of getting a book, and saw her pass along the hall, until she came to the garden door, where she disappeared. I spoke to her as she passed the foot of the stairs, but she did not answer, although as before she stopped and seemed as though *about* to speak.[19]

A very light footstep was sometimes audible during appearances of the apparition and during one evening in August 1884 such footsteps were heard by the family cook and three of Rosina's sisters, all of whom slept on the top landing of the house. Mrs Kinloch, who was sleeping on the ground floor on this particular evening, also heard them. The cook had also seen the figure one evening shortly before, and agreed that the apparition seemed to be dressed in mourning clothes, holding a handkerchief in her right hand. Soon afterwards a neighbour, General Annesley, asked his son to enquire at the Despard household, 'as he had seen a lady crying in our orchard, which is visible from the road. He described her to his son, and afterwards to us, as a tall lady in black, and a bonnet with a long veil, crying, with a handkerchief held up to her face.'[20]

Further appearances of the apparition followed, some of them again in full daylight. Sightings were made by the gardener, the parlourmaid and the three servants in the house, who continued to hear ghostly footsteps while the Despard family was away on holidays. On several occasions, too, the family dogs seemed aware of the apparition's presence.

The following year several visitors and newly appointed servants, some of whom had no prior knowledge of the apparition, also saw it. What is especially interesting about the haunting is that very often the ghostly figure appeared quite solid, although it became 'much less substantial on its later appearances.'

> Up to about 1886 it was so solid and life-like that it was often mistaken for a real person. It actually became less distinct. At all times it intercepted the light; we have not been able to ascertain if it cast a shadow. I should mention that it has been seen through window-glass, and that I myself wear glasses habitually, though none of the other percipients do. The upper part of the figure always left a more distinct impression than the lower, but this may partly be due to the fact that one naturally looks at people's faces before their feet.[21]

It is worth mentioning that on several occasions, after all the other residents of the house had gone to their rooms, Rosina Despard set up a number of fine cords as obstacles across the stairs before going to bed. These cords, fastened by pellets of marine glue, could easily be knocked down by the very lightest touch. 'I have twice at least seen the figure pass through the cords,' wrote Rosina, 'leaving them intact.'

Rosina Despard's account was published in the *Proceedings* of the SPR in 1892 under the pseudonym of Morton. In 1944 a solicitor named George Good wrote to the SPR saying that he had seen a similar apparition but that it was at the Despard family house, not that of the Mortons. He had seen the phantom when he was a small boy, and described it in exactly similar terms as those given above. Even as late as 1958 and 1961, a figure of similar appearance was seen in Cotswold

Lodge – a building, now demolished, which stood across the road from the Despard home and within sight of it.

Rosina Despard believed that the apparition was that of Imogen Swinhoe, the second wife of the first occupant of the house, Henry Swinhoe. She had died at Bristol in 1878 at the age of 41, as the result of dipsomania and sub-acute gastritis, and had been buried in the churchyard of Holy Trinity Church, about 500 yards from her former home.

Crisis Cases

If the Despard sightings are a classic case of a 'haunting' type of apparition, there are also instances where the apparition is seen or heard at the time that the person concerned is undergoing a major crisis – like death. A case of this type is the Bard/de Freville incident where, once again, the apparition appeared quite real. The case was reported by Frederic Myers and is summarized by Andrew MacKenzie in his excellent sourcebook *Hauntings and Apparitions*:

> Alfred Bard was on his way home, and on entering the churchyard at Hinxton, Saffron Walden, Essex, on Friday 8 May 1885, he saw Mrs de Freville, whom he knew well, leaning on the rails of the square stone vault in which her husband was buried, dressed as she normally was in a coal-scuttle bonnet, black jacket with deep crepe, and black dress, but with a face much whiter than usual. She showed awareness of him. He slightly stumbled on a tussock of grass, and when he looked up she was gone. Supposing that she had gone quickly into the tomb he tried to follow her, but the door was shut. Baffled by what had happened, Bard went home and told his wife that he had seen Mrs de Freville. His wife later confirmed this fact. News of Mrs de Freville's death in London was not received in Hinxton until the following day.[22]

Here the crisis of Mrs de Freville's death in London was apparently directly related to the appearance of her apparition near her husband's burial vault in Hinxton and since Mr Bard, the local gardener, was not aware of her actual death at the time, this incident cannot be dismissed as an instance of projected fantasy or imagination.

A somewhat parallel case was investigated by Mrs Eleanor Sidgwick for the SPR. It concerned Lieutenant David McConnel, a trainee pilot, who on 7 December 1918 was asked to fly a Camel aircraft from Scampton to Tadcaster – a distance of 60 miles. McConnel left his room-mate Lieutenant J.J. Larkin at about 11.30 that morning. Then, at around 3.30 pm it seemed that McConnel had returned. The case is summarized by Brian Inglis in his book *The Paranormal*.

> 'The door opened with the usual noise and clatter which David always made. I heard his "Hello boy" and I turned round in my chair and saw him standing in the doorway, dressed in his flying clothes.' They exchanged a few words; 'I was looking at him the whole time he was speaking. He said, "Well, cheerio!", closed the door noisily and went out.' At, or very close to, the time 'David' was visiting his friend, Larkin heard later that day, he had lost control of the aircraft he was flying, crashed and been killed. Describing the episode for the benefit of the SPR, Larkin claimed that although he had heard of such happenings, he had never believed in them. He had always been sceptical; but could be sceptical no longer.[23]

A similar type of crisis apparition appeared before the poet Robert Graves during World War One, while he was serving in northern France. As Graves wrote in *Goodbye to All That*:

> I saw a ghost at Bethune. He was a man called Private Challoner who had been at Lancaster with me, and again at Wrexham. When he went out with a draft to join the First Battalion he shook my hand and said: 'I'll meet you again in France, sir.' He was killed at Festubert in May and in June he passed by our C Company billet where we were just having a special dinner to celebrate our safe return from Cuinchy. There was fish, new potatoes, green peas, asparagus, mutton chops, strawberries and cream, and three bottles of Pommard. Challoner looked in at the window, saluted, and passed on. There was no mistaking him or the cap-badge he was wearing.[24]

Sometimes, however, the crisis associated with the appearance of an apparition is not as severe as death. An interesting SPR case involving a barrister is described by Raymond Bayless in his book *Apparitions and Survival of Death*:

> He was setting at his desk working when he found himself looking at a window pane, and there he saw the face and head of his wife with her eyes closed, her face white, and resting in a reclining position.
>
> When he arrived at his home after working hours, his wife spontaneously told him that she had seen a young niece fall and cut herself and that she, in turn, had fainted. Upon questioning, she said that this fainting incident must have occurred close to two o'clock, which was about the time when her apparition had been seen.
>
> As with all such cases, a telepathic mechanism can be advanced, but it can be seen that the conditions for a projection resulting from shock were present. Interestingly, the fainting woman was wearing a dress which her husband had not seen before but saw correctly on the apparitional form.[25]

Post-Mortem Apparitions

Crisis apparitions and post-mortem apparitions may ostensibly seem to overlap as a category, but when the apparition appears some time after the death has occurred, the 'crisis' component is presumably missing. An interesting example is provided by Dr Elisabeth Kubler-Ross, one of the world's leading authorities on death and dying. In her address 'Death Does Not Exist', presented at the San Diego Holistic Health Conference in 1976,[26] Dr Kubler-Ross described a personal experience of a post-mortem apparition which appeared so real that she initially mistook the phantom image for a living person.

She had been giving her seminars on death and dying at the University of Chicago and she had had a patient, Mrs S., who died two weeks after her son had come of age. Some ten months after this death, Dr Kubler-Ross had begun to feel that her seminars were beginning to lack impetus. A key colleague had recently departed and the current minister on the programme was intent on taking it in a different direction. As a result, on this particular day, Dr Kubler-Ross had decided to give notice that she would leave the University of Chicago and the seminars on death and dying, and pursue her interests elsewhere.

Just as she was confronting the new minister near his office, to tell him of her decision to resign, she noticed the figure of a woman sitting in front of a nearby lift. She seemed somewhat familiar but Dr Kubler-Ross couldn't immediately recall where they had met before. The minister meanwhile departed, and it now dawned on Dr Kubler-Ross that the woman standing before her was an apparition of the mother who had died ten months earlier. She recalled that the apparition was 'very transparent, but not transparent enough that you could see very much behind her.' The woman explained: 'Dr Ross, I had to come back. Do you mind if I walk you to your office? It will only take two minutes.'

Dr Kubler-Ross initially doubted her own perceptions, thinking she must be over-stressed, or experiencing the same sorts of hallucinations as her schizophrenic patients. So she endeavoured to 'touch the skin' of the apparition and kept reminding herself to 'reality-test' events as they walked along the corridor. The apparition now opened Dr Kubler-Ross's door and thanked her for the love and kindness that she and another person, Reverend Gaines, had extended to her while she was alive. As Dr Kubler-Ross sat at her desk, the woman went on to say: 'Your work is not finished. We will help you, and you will know when the time is right, but do not stop now...'

Dr Kubler-Ross was completely dumbfounded by the incident but says that the scientist in her came to the fore. She asked the apparition to write a note in pencil for Reverend Gaines.

> I had no intention of sending this note to my friend, but I needed scientific proof. I mean, somebody who's buried can't write love letters. And this woman, with the most human – no, not human – most loving smile, knowing every thought I had – and I knew, it was thought transference if I've ever experienced it – took this paper and wrote this note, which naturally we have framed in glass and treasure dearly. Then she said, but without words, she said: 'Are you satisfied now?'
>
> I looked at her and thought, I will never be able to share

> this with anybody, but I am going to really hold onto this. Then she got up, ready to leave, repeating 'Dr Ross, you promise,' implying not to give up this work yet. I said, 'I promise.' And the moment I said, 'I promise', she left. We still have her note.[27]

Another interesting post-mortem incident is described by psychiatrist Dr Stanislav Grof in his book *The Adventure of Self-Discovery*. He refers to the tragic accidental death of his friend and colleague Walter Pahnke, who had worked with Grof in experimental LSD research at the Maryland Psychiatric Research Center in Baltimore. Pahnke was interested in parapsychology and had also been friendly with the noted Irish-born psychic medium Eileen Garrett, who had been president of the American Parapsychology Association and was interested in the scientific investigation of *psi* phenomena. As Grof recounts:

> In summer 1971, Walter went with his wife Eva and his children for a vacation in a cabin in Maine, situated right on the ocean. One day, he went scuba-diving all by himself and did not return from the ocean. An extensive and well-organized search failed to find his body or any part of his diving gear. Under these circumstances, Eva found it very difficult to accept and integrate his death. Her last memory of Walter when he was leaving the cabin involved him full of energy and in perfect health. It was hard for her to believe that he was not part of her life any more and to start a new chapter of her existence without a sense of closure of the preceding one.
>
> Being a psychologist herself, she qualified for an LSD training session for mental health professionals offered through a special program in our institute. She decided to have a psychedelic experience with the hope of getting some more insights and asked me to be her sitter. In the second half of the session, she had a very powerful vision of Walter and carried on a long and meaningful dialogue with him. He gave her specific instructions concerning each of their three children and released her to start a new life of her own, unencumbered and unrestricted by a sense of commitment to his memory. It was a very profound and liberating experience.

Just as Eva was questioning whether the entire episode was just a wishful fabrication of her own mind, Walter appeared once more for a brief period of time with the following request: 'I forgot one thing. Would you please do me a favor and return a book that I borrowed from a friend of mine. It is in the study in the attic.' And he proceeded to give her the name of the friend, the name of the book, the shelf, and the sequential order of the book on this shelf. Following the instructions, Eva was actually able to find and return the book, about the existence of which she had had no previous knowledge.

It would certainly have been completely consistent with Walter's lifelong search for a scientific proof of paranormal phenomena to add a concrete and testable piece of information to his interaction with Eva to dispel her doubts.[28]

Apparitional cases of the Pahnke type are sometimes referred to as 'informational cases'. Celia Green and Charles McCreery of the Institute of Psychophysical Research in Oxford provide an example of the apparition of a deceased grandfather who seems to have appeared in order to warn the family about the dangerous escape of gas in their family home.

I work in a mill; one night on returning home I had a feeling of slight tummy upset and headache. I decided to have an early night in bed. I put my husband's dinner in the gas oven on a low light to be ready about ten o'clock when he came home. I went out to the coal bunker and banked the fire up also. Then I retired to bed. I must have slept for about three hours when I wakened up suddenly to see my 'dead' Grandfather stood by my bedside. He had his back to me, and was looking over his shoulder at me. I could see everything else in the room. It did not appear to be a dream. I could see plainly his snow-white hair just hanging over the top of his macintosh. I could see the wrinkles on the cloth as he stood there. Just looking at me; he looked so real I eventually stretched out my hand to touch him, and, immediately the apparition sort of broke up and melted away. I was dumbfounded. Why, I asked myself, should I 'see' my Grandfather when he had been dead so long ago. My mother had died so much more recently. Thoroughly awakened now by this unexplained happening I decided to go down and take a look at the dinner in the oven. As I went downstairs and opened the door at the bottom I gasped. The house reeked of gas. I opened all the doors and turned off the gas. I can only assume that when I went for the coal, on shutting the back door the draught had blown the gas out. I have always thought since that somehow he came to *warn* me. It puzzled me so much as to why it should have been Grandfather I saw, when I had not seen him since I was a girl of fifteen. I was then forty-seven. *He looked so really alive*, although he did not speak. I could not smell gas until I went downstairs.[29]

Experimental Cases

Professor Arthur Ellison describes an experimental-type apparition as 'one in which someone is deliberately trying to make his or her apparition visible to a percipient and succeeds in doing so'. Clearly this category of apparitions relates to the living not the dying, and there is a degree of overlap here with classical OBE cases. The following instance of a 'willed' apparition, like the gas incident above, is from the archives of the Institute of Psychophysical Research.

I thought just recently that I would try to see my eldest son living in Rhodesia. For five nights just before I fell asleep, I willed very strongly that I would be allowed to 'see Charles in Rhodesia'. On the sixth night, I almost forgot to put my mind to the matter, and being almost asleep I just thought 'I wish I could see Charles', not mentioning Rhodesia. I was just beginning to wake up about 7.45 am when suddenly I found myself in the living room, seated on the settee, which had by some means been pushed back against the wall, so that I had a clear view of the door. I had a great feeling of elation and knew that some Being was clearing the way as it were; the whole atmosphere seemed to be in motion. Presently I heard hurrying footsteps, and knowing it was morning I thought my eldest daughter must have come back home, instead of going on to College. The footsteps drew nearer still hurrying, but I now realised that it was a man's footsteps I could hear. Suddenly the door opened, and a man's head and shoulders appeared: I thought at first it was

> that of one of my brothers whom I had not seen for some years, then to my delight I realised it was Charles, five years older than when I last saw him and very lean and brown; his skin much darker than I would have expected. He looked around the room impatiently, and with a very surprised look on his face; he must have wondered what on earth he was doing there, as he has never seen this flat and he did not turn round far enough to see me, though I willed it with all my heart. I knew that this was a gift, and the moment would soon be gone; so I eagerly took in every aspect of his features and clothing. In another moment I was back in bed.[30]

In some instances like this it is possible that the 'apparition' may be a hallucinated form within an imagined environment, the details being constructed from memory or anticipated sensory impressions. Unfortunately we have no record of what Charles 'saw' at the time of his mother's willed projection of consciousness. However, on other occasions of willed projection there has been some corroborative evidence. The following is an account written by Mr S.H. Beard, an acquaintance of Sir William Barrett of the Society for Psychical Research:

> On Friday December 1st 1882 at 9.30 pm I went into a room alone and sat by the fireside, and endeavoured so strongly to fix my mind upon the interior of a house at Kew...in which resided Miss Verity and her two sisters, that I seemed to be actually in the house. During this experiment I must have fallen into a mesmeric sleep for...I could not move my limbs...At 10 pm I regained my normal state by an effort of will and...wrote down the foregoing statements. When I went to bed on this same night, I determined that I would be in the front bedroom of the above-mentioned house at 12 midnight and remain there until I had made my spiritual presence perceptible to the inmates of that room.
>
> On the next day, Saturday, I went to Kew to spend the evening and met there a married sister of Miss Verity, namely Mrs L [whom he had met only once before]. In the course of conversation...she told me that on the previous night she had seen me distinctly on two occasions...At about half-past nine she had seen me in the passage going from one room to another, and at midnight when she was wide awake she had seen me enter the bedroom...and take her hair into

my hand...She then awoke her sister, Miss Verity, who was sleeping with her and told her about it.[31]

Explaining Apparitions

As the Society for Psychical Research began to accumulate a large body of anecdotal data related to apparitions and hauntings, so too several prominent psychical researchers endeavoured to make sense of the material they had collected. In due course five hypotheses emerged.

The first model, advocated by Edmund Gurney, regarded apparitions as mental hallucinations created in response to telepathic impulses received from the individual involved. On the other hand, G.N.M. Tyrrell considered apparitions to be 'idea patterns' emanating from the subconscious mind of the percipient, with or without the involvement of the psyche of the other subject. A third view, advanced by Frederic Myers, Raynor Johnson and others, held that apparitions were 'etheric images' related to mental events in the past or present. The fourth, 'occult', model supported the concept of projected 'astral' or 'etheric' bodies as the basis of apparitional appearances, while the Spiritualists regarded apparitions of the dead simply as spirits of departed souls and proof of post-mortem survival.

These prevailing theories of apparitions were evaluated in turn by the American sociologist Professor Hornell Hart and several other collaborators in a paper entitled 'Six Theories About Apparitions', published in the *Proceedings* of the SPR 1953–6. Here Hart and his colleagues endeavoured to produce a coherent overview that drew on different aspects of each of the existing models. Two basic propositions were advanced:

1. Apparitions and their accessories are semi-*substantial* in the sense that they tend to have the following characteristics:

(a) they are described as 'solid', 'real', or the like, and their visible details are often said to be vivid;
(b) they are often perceived tactually and audibly as well as visibly, and these three kinds of perception are consistent with one another;
(c) as thus perceived, they appear to be recognizably

similar to – and often identical with – material human bodies and physical objects;

(d) their observed details may be otherwise unknown to any living person, and yet may prove to be verifiably correct;

(e) they make adjustments to their physical surroundings and to physically embodied people, in much the same ways in which physically present people would do;

(f) they are seen in normal perspective, both when stationary and when moving; they may be reflected in mirrors, may obscure other objects and be obscured by other objects, and in other ways they fit into the physical environment as physical objects do;

(g) they are often seen collectively by two or more persons at the same time.

2. Apparitions and their accessories are only *semi*-substantial in the sense that they tend to have the following characteristics:

(a) their visibility is erratic, in that they are likely to appear or disappear suddenly and inexplicably, to be invisible to people who would see them if they were physically embodied, to fade in or out, and to be self-luminous;

(b) they may pass through solid walls or locked doors;

(c) they may rise into the air without physical support, and may glide instead of walk;

(d) they may communicate without words, gestures or other symbols – in other words, telepathically.

The model advanced by Hart was a modified 'etheric' theory which assumed that all living creatures had an 'etheric double'. It also assumed that etheric objects could be created by the imagination and have their own semi-tangible existence – a variation on the 'thought-forms' of the Theosophists. Professor H.H. Price of Oxford University had a similar idea in mind when he noted that some hauntings might be the result of mental images lingering in psychic space with apparently dynamic properties of their own.

Following on from the Hart study, Dr Robert Crookall, a prolific collector of OBE and apparition cases, made a more specific distinction between what he called the 'vehicle of vitality' and the 'soul body'.[32] According to Crookall only the soul body could operate as a vehicle for consciousness so that when it was observed in an apparitional form it could demonstrate intelligence and 'communicate'. The vehicle of vitality, on the other hand, was made of a type of 'ectoplasmic' or 'ideoplastic' substance capable of change by the powers of thought, and it was this ectoplasm which psychic mediums were able to observe clairvoyantly as a type of vaporous mist. Apparitions based on the projection of this 'vehicle of vitality' would be non-conscious: simply thought forms drifting around in psychic space like automatons.

Crookall also believed that the amount of 'ectoplasm' projected affected the 'density' of the apparition. Some projected doubles with a large percentage of ectoplasm would have difficulty passing through walls and other physical barriers but, for the same reason, could cause physical effects of the poltergeist type (moving objects, creating sounds etc.) Crookall also maintained that some apparitions could combine both the 'vital' and 'soul-body' elements, and that this would vary in degree from case to case.

Although at first glance Dr Crookall's concept sounds somewhat complicated, I believe that it is quite possibly the best model advanced to far. It is supported by the first-hand data of such pragmatic OBE projectors as Robert Monroe and also provides us with a useful distinction between pure human consciousness and the thought forms created by the human imagination. Potentially, too, it allows us to understand the role that mythic and archetypal imagery - and belief systems in general - might play in the various realms of after-death consciousness. Indeed, we are left with the prospect that the act of dying might well unfold the most remarkable range of visionary experiences that we could possibly imagine!

5.

In Search of New Paradigms

A key task which confronts transpersonal and paranormal researchers is to make sense of the vast accumulation of data on visionary consciousness which now challenges many of our preconceptions about 'reality'. As we have seen, many different sorts of people can be visionaries – artists, mystics, psychologists, hospital victims, founders of religion. These are the people who in various ways and often in quite different circumstances have achieved a major experiential break-through: a radical shift in consciousness which has provided access to more profound domains of inner spiritual knowledge. Sometimes this visionary perception has revealed states of ecstasy and transcendence, sometimes it has summoned the devils and demons from the darker recesses of the mind. But in all instances the borders of normal consciousness have been crossed and in many instances the boundaries between subject and object have dissolved altogether.

So what is this nebulous, elusive thing we call visionary consciousness? How are we to understand mystical revelations, NDEs and OBE perception? And what of the accumulated evidence relating to apparitions and phantoms? Do they belong in the same terrain? Are all these phenomena part of an experiential domain that lies beyond the spectrum of everyday awareness? It seems to me to be quite crucial that we resolve issues like these if we are to have any understanding of who we are and what we are doing here on earth. For without incorporating mystical and paranormal data of this sort into our paradigm of reality it is quite clear that our psychologies and philosophies – our attempts at an integrated world-view – must necessarily be shallow and incomplete.

It may now be useful to summarize some of the principal themes in the OBE, NDE and apparition data and relate them to models of human consciousness itself.

First, there seems to be substantial evidence that some form of ethereal body survives death and becomes the continuing vehicle of consciousness. Several OBE and NDE subjects report that they have actually observed the gradual dissociation of the vehicle of consciousness from the physical body and that this 'consciousness' seems to be the source of their real identity. So the implication remains, as different spiritual traditions have maintained over the centuries, that we do indeed have a 'soul' and that this resides within the physical organism while we are alive.

The fact that OBE and NDE subjects are able to observe their surroundings at a distance from their bodies, and often from a completely different but nevertheless coherent perspective, suggests that this vehicle of consciousness has faculties of perception akin to those we make use of in our physical bodies, and maybe that we have 'bodies within the body' that perform parallel functions when dissociated from each other. Sometimes, as we have noted, normal perceptual constraints associated with physical awareness are removed altogether - some OBE/NDE subjects have reported 360° vision in the dissociated state, and according to Elisabeth Kubler-Ross and Herbert Greenhouse there are also cases of people with impaired vision being able to see perfectly in the out-of-the-body state.[1]

This ethereal body, or vehicle of consciousness, is also able to move and act through the power of thought, and it may well be that where the spirit form is perceived by others as resembling the normal physical form, this is the result of the individual consciousness drawing on familiar stereotypes and 'creating' them in an imaginal way. When the astral counterpart is not seen as clothed or semi-physical, it is normally described in indeterminate terms - as a 'luminous glow', as a body of light, as a field of energy, and so on. In general terms, even where there is no specific awareness of body image, OBE and NDE subjects still perceive their environment as if they had a body, and to this extent retain a sense of continuing individuality. However in the OBE state we sometimes find imaginal forms inhabiting the same psychic terrain as more familiar 'physical' forms. Oliver Fox and Robert Monroe have both reported 'mythic' or 'religious' imagery as part of the OBE, and Monroe says he has also observed discarnate beings confined psychically within an emotionally created perceptual domain which to all intents and purposes restricts the field of consciousness for that person.

This 'emotional field' may in fact be illusory within a broader context, but it remains profoundly real to the person experiencing it on this level of awareness. So there is a clear implication that in post-mortem states of being, human consciousness may find itself surrounded by imaginal constructs directly related to the individual's emotional and mental condition at the time of death. Allan Lewis and several other NDE subjects have alluded to the type of limbo world that suicide victims find themselves entering after death, and Dr George Ritchie's report of discarnate beings seeking to perpetuate their alcoholic fixation in the spirit realm is also a case in point.

It may well be that certain instances of haunting apparitions are in fact discarnate human intelligences trapped within an imaginal energy-field created through some sort of emotional or physical crisis that was related to their death. The person who observes such an apparition – usually while they are themselves in an altered state of consciousness (a state of relaxation, near-sleep, sensory deprivation, night-vision etc.) may then observe not only the individual spirit form but the entire scenario connected with the crisis, these images being an integral part of the psychic field of the traumatized individual.

The Tibetan Book of the Dead and other cosmological works of a similar nature have a lot to say about mythic and supernatural beings which we can now understand as projections of the psyche, but which emanate from more exalted levels of spiritual consciousness than those thought forms associated with the more basic emotions. Most OBE and apparition cases lack this transcendent dimension and reflect a perceptual domain largely related to the physical world as we know it. Similarly, in the NDE literature there are numerous cases where the subjects have a predominantly physical frame of reference, as with the woman who observed, while in her dissociative state, a tennis shoe located high up on a window ledge. It is only in those instances that are profoundly 'eschatological', to use D. Scott

Rogo's term, that a much more transcendent or 'spiritual' domain becomes apparent and the subject meets deceased relatives, experiences mystical visions, has encounters with archetypal beings or becomes inspired by the divine grace of God.

It would seem, then, that there is a spectrum of consciousness from substantially physical forms through to mystical and transcendent states of awareness and that these may become increasingly accessible in the various dissociative states. Insofar as 'consciousness' itself is concerned, the crucial difference between a person who is physically alive and one who is operating in non-physical realms of being is that the live person has a more restricted spectrum of awareness because there are more 'filters' through which his determinants of 'reality' have to pass. While he is occupying a physical organism his frameworks of perception are based substantially on cues passing to his brain through the normal sensory channels and in this way – as we mentioned in the first chapter of this book – his concept of physical reality is built up and reinforced. It is only during periodic altered states of consciousness (dreams, visions, peak experiences, OBEs, NDEs) that the broader spectrum of psychic and spiritual imagery is revealed. In the dissociative state, however, as we have already noted, it is possible for the individual's perceptual domain to combine 'physical' elements with a potentially vast range of emotional, psychical and mythic imagery. In such circumstances the individual may well find himself in a heaven or hell substantially of his own making.

Transpersonal Approaches to Mystical Consciousness

Somewhat surprisingly, the main proponents of transpersonal frameworks of consciousness have tended to understate or ignore the cumulative body of paranormal evidence in presenting their models of the mind. Historically, transpersonal maps of altered states have derived either from the psychedelic research undertaken during the late 1960s and early 1970s, or from frameworks based substantially on eastern religious traditions. While I would certainly not dispute the very considerable contribution that Hindu and Buddhist concepts have made to transpersonal thought, it seems to me that ultimately the most complete frameworks of mystical and visionary consciousness will be those which transcend specific belief systems altogether.

At this particular time in history we are fortunate indeed to have the happy coincidence of an advanced medical technology that has made possible the systematic recording of NDE cases, coupled with the pragmatic exploration of OBE states undertaken by people like Robert Monroe. In short, we are beginning to accumulate a real body of data on dissociative and 'peak' states of consciousness which in turn have a direct bearing on the authenticity of religious beliefs. We may well be entering a new phase where religious and mystical experiences can be demystified and subjected to some sort of testing and validation. Without doubt, a new pragmatism has appeared on the horizon.

It needs to be said, though, that to date it has been extremely difficult to evaluate visionary and mystical consciousness without some recourse to existing cultural frameworks and belief systems. For example, Ken Wilber's 'Spectrum of Consciousness' model has been profoundly influenced by Vajrayana Buddhism and Vedanta, John Lilly's framework, outlined in *The Centre of the Cyclone*, was based substantially on the Gurdjieff/Oscar Ichazo teachings, Daniel Goleman's 'Map for Inner Space' derived from the Buddhist *Abhidhamma* and *Visuddhimagga* texts and Professor R.C. Zaehner's concept of 'authentic' mysticism was clearly coloured by his own Roman Catholic beliefs. Meanwhile the famous 'manual for spiritual rebirth' compiled by Timothy Leary, Richard Alpert and Ralph Metzner – *The Psychedelic Experience* – was substantially based on *The Tibetan Book of the Dead*.

Not all transpersonal models have had this type of orientation, however. Some frameworks have evolved from humanistic psychology, including Stanislav Grof's exploration of perinatal matrices in altered states of consciousness and Roland Fischer's cartography of ecstatic states. Most approaches, however, have tended to ignore the implications of current OBE/NDE evidence and its parallels with classical shamanism. And the latter is especially relevant since, as a visionary approach to mystical consciousness *par excellence*, its basic techniques may be employed without any substantial cultural overlay. I will come back to this issue later, but at this point it will be useful to compare some of the main transpersonal approaches to mystical consciousness for the insights they provide in evaluating visionary reality.

It is a fact of history that the Human Potential Movement and its most recent manifestation, transpersonal psychology, derived much of its early data on altered states of consciousness from psychedelic research. Not surprisingly, some of the earliest debates about mystical consciousness focused very much on what was 'authentic' and what was 'artificial' in the pursuit of 'chemical ecstasy'.

The debate had been triggered initially by the publication in 1954 of Aldous Huxley's *The Doors of Perception*. Huxley even took his title from William Blake's pronouncement that 'if the doors of perception were cleansed, everything would appear to man as it is, infinite'. Huxley related how in May 1953 he had swallowed four-tenths of a gram of mescalin dissolved in a glass of water and sat down to wait for the results. For Huxley, mescalin brought revelation: his 'I' became 'Not-Self' and the everyday objects around him – flowers, books and furniture – seemed to radiate jewel-like colours and profound significance. Here, he felt, was 'contemplation at its height'. Huxley later conceded that mescalin could plunge some people into hell rather than lifting them up to heaven, but on balance he decided that it could certainly be a catalyst to mystical awareness – especially for rational or 'verbal' intellectuals like himself who felt 'compelled to take an occasional trip through some chemical Door in the Wall into the world of transcendental experience'. Later, in 1958, in *The Saturday Evening Post*, Huxley emphasized the mystical relevance of both mescalin and the more recently discovered psychedelic, LSD. Of LSD he wrote: 'It lowers the barrier between conscious and subconscious and permits the patient to look more deeply and understandingly into the recesses of his own mind. The deepening of self-knowledge takes place against a background of visionary and even mystical experience.'[2]

But if Aldous Huxley and later Timothy Leary, Gerald Heard, Alan Watts and beat poet Allen Ginsberg seemed to be advocating chemical catalysts as a path to authentic mystical awareness, there were others who disagreed. R.C. Zaehner, Professor of Eastern Religions and Ethics at Oxford University, argued strongly against this viewpoint in his book *Mysticism, Sacred and Profane*, published in 1957. Zaehner branded Huxley's viewpoint as 'absurd arrogance' which had no connection with 'the direct experience of God in his unutterable holiness'. Nevertheless, while Zaehner argued that, for the Christian, mystical experience would be characterized by a state of consciousness 'in which the soul feels itself to be united with God by love', he grudgingly conceded that Huxley's experience of the 'Not-Self' bore some resemblance to Henry Suso's Christian writings on 'melting into the will of God and the abandonment of self'. Zaehner's real reservation, it seems to me, was that Huxley's explorations hinted at a possible relationship between mysticism and psychosis, and for Zaehner this would have posed a very distinct challenge to his own, committed belief system. As we have seen, though, and as Huxley himself conceded, as human beings we all have the capacity to enter a visionary heaven or hell which reflects the personal and archetypal contents of our minds. Traditional cosmologies in both eastern and western religion similarly present us with very clear symbolic depictions of the polarity between harmony and disunity, good and evil - so such a finding should have come as no surprise to Zaehner.

The psychedelic era, both in the United States and elsewhere in the western world, was a time of tumultuous social upheaval and elicited a wide spectrum of emotional responses from different factions in the political and intellectual hierarchy. These days one can look at the psychedelic debate in a more dispassionate way. And yet the debate itself may not be over: there is once again renewed interest in serious psychedelic research in California, as exemplified by the founding of the Albert Hofmann Foundation,[3] and the 1990s may well herald a revival of 1960s consciousness, while hopefully on a more integrated and socially responsible level. This aside, most systematic approaches to mystical consciousness which have developed within the Human Potential Movement in recent years do not take sides on this particular issue.

One of the earliest models of consciousness to flow from the psychedelic era was put forward by neurophysiologist Dr John Lilly, and in turn combined elements from the systems of Oscar Ichazo and Gurdjieff. Ichazo used Gurdjieffian 'vibrational numbers' to specify states of consciousness, and these could be conceived as both positive and negative vibrational levels.[4] Lilly listed ± 48 as a 'neutral' human biocomputer state, appropriate for the reception of new ideas, and then envisaged a positive and negative hierarchy of consciousness, polarizing in two directions. On the negative side, at – 24 for example, one might experience pain, guilt and fear and then this might intensify at – 12 as migraine. In – 6 one could experience extreme guilt and meaninglessness – a type of purgatory – while in – 3, as Lilly put it, 'one is fused with other entities throughout the universe but these are all bad...this is the quintessence of evil, the deepest hell of which one can conceive.

On the positive vibrationary scale, however, a more optimistic outcome was possible. In + 24 one entered a state of basically pleasurable activities which in + 12 then intensified into bliss, grace and heightened bodily awareness. In + 6 one became a 'point of consciousness' and might fuse with other entities, while in + 3 one entered Classical Satori. Lilly defined this as 'Fusion with universal mind, Union with God, being one of the Creators of energy from the Void'.

Lilly's model remains a pertinent construct and acknowledges the distinct polarities of consciousness which clearly prevail in altered states. However this classification of 'astral travel' as a + 6 activity requires some modification, since there are varying degrees of transcendence in the out-of-the-body state.

Daniel Goleman first outlined his 'Map of Inner Space' in his book *The Varieties of the Meditative Experience*, published in 1977, and it has also appeared in a condensed form in various 'consciousness' anthologies as well as in his more recent work *The Meditative Mind*. Here he presented the Buddhist *Abhidhamma* as 'probably the broadest and most detailed traditional psychology of states of consciousness'. In the fifth century AD, the monk Buddhaghosa condensed the sections of the *Abhidhamma* relating to meditation into the *Visuddhimagga*, or Path to Purification, thus providing a type of manual for meditation. Goleman's framework is essentially a map of consciousness states that can be attained through Buddhist meditation.

As Goleman notes, initially a meditator's mind tends to wander from its object and 'one-pointedness' is only attained spasmodically. Gradually the meditator gains increasing control, overcoming mental habits antagonistic to the task.

According to Goleman the first major attainment in meditation is a state in which all distractions are subdued and the meditator enters a state of 'access' concentration. 'At this access level,' he writes, 'strong feelings of zest or rapture emerge, along with happiness, pleasure and equanimity...there may also be a sensation of lightness, as though the body were floating in the air.'

Goleman also says that visions may begin to appear at this point and that they can be frightening or benign. However he cautions that a 'danger to the meditator is becoming enraptured by beatific visions and so halting further progress by making them the goal of one's meditation...The meditator's goal is beyond visions...'

In the system outlined in the *Visuddhimagga* one continues to meditate until there is a break from normal awareness and consciousness is not dominated by 'rapture, bliss and one-pointedness'. Full mastery, says Goleman, 'comes when the meditator can attain *jhana* whenever, wherever, as soon as, and for as long as he wishes.' *Jhanas* are states of 'full absorption' where the mind 'suddenly seems to sink into the object and remains fixed in it.'

In due course the meditator enters four 'formless' states and increasingly turns his attention towards 'infinite non-existence'. The final *jhana* is a state of 'neither perception nor non-perception'. Here, says Goleman, 'No mental states are decisively present. Their residuals remain, though they are nearly absent. This state approaches the ultimate limit of perception.'

The *Visuddhimagga* does not merely present a structure of consciousness, however, for as Goleman emphasizes, a sense of discriminating wisdom is also vital. In particular he notes that one must learn to transcend 'pseudo-Nirvana' – meditative attachment to brilliant lights, rapturous feelings, tranquil body sensations and even the sheer clarity of thought which flows from these states of consciousness. True Nirvana lies beyond all of these, for here 'awareness of all physical and mental phenomena ceases entirely'.

A more complex framework of consciousness, and one regarded by many as the central benchmark of transpersonal thought, is that proposed by Ken Wilber. Like John Lilly,

Wilber has found himself drawn to a hierarchical model of consciousness. According to Wilber, each level of the mind reveals ever greater differentiation so that, with each higher level of consciousness new structures – faculties and potentials – emerge which encompass and control the lower levels but also extend beyond them. Wilber thus believes that hierarchical structure is basic to the very nature of the mind and that in the process of gaining transcendence, the ego must 'die' on one level before ascending to the next.

In following a non-dualistic viewpoint Wilber believes that one's true self is nothing other than *Brahman* or The Void – as represented in Hinduism and Buddhism respectively – and that the mental ego is essentially illusory. The final goal of human development is thus to eliminate the illusion of the self and transcend it.

In his essay 'Psychologia Perennis: The Spectrum of Consciousness', Wilber summarizes his core concepts by presenting human personality as 'a multi-levelled manifestation or expression of a single Consciousness, just as in physics the electro-magnetic spectrum is viewed as a multi-banded expression of a single, characteristic electro-magnetic wave'.[5]

Following the perennial wisdom tradition of the East, Wilber maintains that man's innermost consciousness 'is identical to the absolute and ultimate reality of the universe' and he represents this as 'mind': 'Mind is what there is and all there is, spaceless and therefore infinite, timeless and therefore eternal, outside of which nothing exists.' The other levels of consciousness on the spectrum, accordingly, are different degrees of illusion, or *Maya*, and as Wilber notes, 'Maya is any experience constituted by, or stemming from, dualism.'

The 'lowest' level of Wilber's spectrum is a stage of consciousness he calls the 'Shadow', where man identifies with an impoverished self-image and has repressed part of his psyche as 'alien', 'evil' or 'undesirable'. To this extent Wilber follows Carl Jung quite closely.

On the next level of 'Ego', the individual identifies with a mental image of himself but perceives himself to exist' *in* his body and not *as* his body'. This, for Wilber, is a substantially intellectual level of reality.

At the next level in Wilber's hierarchy – the existential level – man identifies with his 'total psychophysical organism'. Wilber would say that here there has been a profound development towards individual integration because the person now accepts all facets of his or her total organism. He quotes Gestalt therapist Fritz Perls as embodying this process: 'Lose your mind and come to your senses!'

Wilber recognizes, though, that beyond the individual level of psychophysical awareness and at a higher existential level lie 'Biosocial Bands' of consciousness. Here we are considering the individual in the context of society. But social patterns filter our capacity for feeling and perceiving into culturally acceptable modes, so to this extent such cultural patterns distort or restrict consciousness. They do so because all societies consist of people in relationships and a certain amount of social cohesion and stability is required. However, as a consequence, human consciousness is prevented from attaining complete self-realization.

At the transpersonal levels of the spectrum we come to a perceptual domain where consciousness is able to transcend the individual level but still, as Wilber puts it, 'is not yet completely identified with the All.' This is the level of the Jungian archetypes, of mythic primordial consciousness. It is interesting to note that Jung himself defined mystical experience as 'experience of archetypes'. At the transpersonal level of consciousness on Wilber's spectrum, the individual is able to witness the 'transcendent' and 'miraculous', and this is a profoundly spiritual realm of being, but it remains dualistic because even here individual awareness still persists.

For Wilber, and in accordance with Vedanta and Mahayana Buddhist non-dualism, the supreme level is reached when Mind alone exists: when there is no distinction whatever between subject and object.

> The individual goes right to the very bottom of his being to find who or what is doing the seeing and he *ultimately* finds – instead of a transpersonal self – nothing other than what is seen, which Blyth called 'the experience by the universe of the universe'.

As mentioned earlier, other humanistic cartographers of inner space have arrived at their models without specific reference to religious and spiritual belief systems. Prominent among these are Stanislav Grof and Roland Fischer.

Grof's approach to altered states of consciousness, conceived originally as a result of extensive LSD research and more recently with non-psychedelic Holotropic Breathing methods, deals, like Wilber's, with pathways to transpersonal states and Unity Consciousness and also acknowledges the awesome spiritual archetypes encountered during 'rebirth' experiences. Grof is also interested to explore levels of the mind where a profound sense of interconnectedness is experienced by the individual – where there is a sense of unity not only with 'God' or 'The Light' or 'Infinite Space' but also with other forms and beings in the universe. At certain levels of transcendence, says Grof, feelings of individual separateness and distinctiveness seem to fall away:

> Here the mandatory boundaries of the body seem to be melting and the person has the experience, perhaps, of fusing with other people, or becoming other people, becoming animals, becoming plant life and in some cases having telepathic experiences. Sometimes, too, there are mythological or archetypal sequences, portraying something that this culture would not normally regard as part of objective reality or the phenomenal world.[6]

Elaborating on his last point, Grof has also commented:

> There exists a group of paranormal phenomena that can be described...as extensions of consciousness within the framework of 'objective reality'. In the case of precognition, clairvoyance and clairaudience, astral projection, 'time travel' and telepathy, it again is not the content of these experiences that is extraordinary, but the way of acquiring certain information or perceiving a certain situation that according to common sense and the existing scientific paradigms should be beyond reach.[7]

Grof's emphasis is rather different from Wilber's, which tends to portray ego-dissolution rather than universal connectedness as the ultimate reality. However, Grof has noted that some of his LSD subjects have had 'the most generalised and universal experiences of this kind [which] involve identification with the consciousness of the Universal Mind and with the Supracosmic and Metacosmic Void'.

Finally, it is appropriate to mention Roland Fischer's

'cartography of ecstatic and meditative states' which at first glance seems markedly different from the models summarized above.

Fischer's model initially offers us two different 'directions' or polarities of consciousness. These appear mutually exclusive at first but eventually meet at the same juncture, as if one is journeying around the circumference of a circle from different directions. One of the directions is characterized by increased perceptual arousal, the other by decreased arousal.

In one direction the spectrum ranges from normal awareness through various states of 'ergotropic' arousal of the sympathetic nervous system. This part of Fischer's spectrum helps us to understand, for example, what happens during a psychedelic hallucinatory 'trip'. Here the individual passes through various degrees of enhanced sensitivity, creativity and anxiety and these in turn can lead to a schizophrenic or catatonic condition, or open out into mystical rapture. Fischer regards enhanced creativity as a type of superior data processing, and notes that schizophrenics are people who are simply not able to integrate the contents of the psychic worlds they inhabit. However, at the peak of ecstatic rapture, says Fischer, the outside physical world 'retreats to the fringe of consciousness' and the individual reflects himself in his own 'program'. Elsewhere Fischer explains what he means by a 'program':

> During the ecstatic state, there is neither capacity nor necessity for motor verification of the intense sensations. In the mental dimension, in contrast to the physical, the all-pervasive experience of absolute certainty does not require further verification and will be structured according to the current mythology or the belief system of a St Francis, Pascal or Ramakrishna. What is one man's loss of freedom, therefore, may be another's gain in creativity.[8]

Travelling in the other direction on Fischer's spectrum of consciousness, we move along a 'trophotropic' continuum which takes us from normal awareness into progressive states of relaxation, deep meditation and in due course, Yoga *Samadhi*. For Fischer, however, whether we go on this path or on the path of heightened arousal, we arrive at the same place, since the 'self' of ecstasy and the 'self' of *Samadhi* are one and the same 'Self'. 'In the Self-state of ecstasy and Samadhi,' he says, 'cortical and subcortical activity are indistinguishably integrated. This unity is reflected in the experience of Oneness with everything, a Oneness with the universe that is oneself.'[9]

So, according to Fischer, whichever direction we headed off on initially in our venture into altered states of consciousness, we inevitably moved away from normal awareness which depends upon the distinction between subject and object for our sanity and survival. However, we finally arrive at a state of awareness where the 'separation of object and subject gradually disappears and their interaction becomes the principal content of the experience'.

All of these major models of consciousness have much to commend them, and in different ways each throws light on specific aspects of altered states. Lilly's model reminds us of the vibratory polarity of the visionary experience – how heavenly symbolism can suddenly reveal its dark or hellish side, how panic can engulf ecstasy in these rarefied realms of perception. Fischer, too, draws a much-needed distinction between the 'hallucinatory' mystical path which initially intensifies the encounter with psychic imagery and then transcends that domain, and the meditative route to *Samadhi* which takes us through states of deep relaxation to levels beyond thought-content itself. However, as Fischer points out – although Zaehner would no doubt disagree – both pathways seem to lead to the same state of ecstasy. Fischer's approach is also a pleasing departure from the more static and linear models of consciousness and is among the most dynamic offered so far.

Goleman's meditative framework deals essentially with one-pointedness of mind and the progressive path of individual consciousness towards the Void, which no doubt is authentic enough as a statement of Buddhist mystical intent but seems to ignore many details of the perceptual universe which we have discussed elsewhere in this book. Admittedly, all visionary content in the psyche is in the final analysis 'illusory' if one takes the Buddhist position, but that does not greatly assist our cause: there is a vast region of archetypal, mythic and biographical material in the psyche through which we will all have to pass *en route* to the Void, and it is worthwhile, it seems to me, to chart the terrain.

Also, by comparison with Fischer's model, Goleman's seems somewhat one-sided. There are many pathways up the mountain which lead toward ecstatic union with the Godhead, and the *Visuddhimagga* is undoubtedly one of them: a literally clear-sighted mystical path which has as its goal the conquest of dualism. However, some may find this approach too Spartan despite its authenticity. Because of the obsession with *Maya* in the East, many Hindu and Buddhist models of altered states seem to be lacking in detail when it comes to describing the transitional realms. The experiential traveller from a western intellectual background may well find that additional material from the esoteric and psychedelic literature is required, especially in exploring the maze of the western psyche.

The same point, it seems to me, can be made about Ken Wilber's 'Spectrum of Consciousness'. While authentically based as a framework of non-dualism, its structures seem on closer analysis to be too cerebral to be completely convincing. Does the universe really consist of neatly defined constructs and processes, of specific stages and levels? Somehow the dynamism – the sheer awesomeness of metaphysical consciousness and the rich poetic tapestry of archetypal imagery – is missing in models like this. My quarrel is not with Wilber's intent, because many of the major mystical traditions – not only Buddhism and Hinduism but the Kabbalah as well – have us heading towards the Infinite Void that transcends form and appearance.

But structures tend to imply their own sense of certainty. We are inclined to forget, after all, that models and maps of visionary consciousness are only that: they draw finally on metaphors and symbols and allusions. So eventually the maps must be enriched by the personal accounts of the travellers who have actually undergone these profound and subtle processes of human transformation. It is easy enough to talk of *totally* dissolving the ego in the Void but has anyone really done it and returned to tell the tale? Meanwhile we must continue to plot upon the chart of consciousness those accounts of out-of-the-body travellers, Gnostic venturers in the spirit and assorted shamans, mystics and creative visionaries who have journeyed through the various levels of *Maya* which precede the great absorption into Unity Consciousness. This is the sort of information we really need. It is not so much the final destination – most major mystical traditions are in substantial agreement about that – but the complex transformative journey and the visionary encounters we must undergo to get there.

My feeling, therefore, is that the structures of consciousness proposed within the transpersonal movement so far need to be enriched with more human content: we need more personal accounts from the people who have explored these psychic and spiritual territories and who can then help us with the details we require to enlarge our maps and models. This is why the experiential data from paranormal research and the visionary techniques of shamanism are so valuable.

A Paranormal Model of Consciousness

An initial point that can be made about the emphasis on non-dualism in the other frameworks discussed here is that non-dualism itself is hardly pertinent as a mystical concept until the final attainment of Unity Consciousness. Until this transcendent level of awareness is reached – and most, if not all, visionary explorers fall far short of this sort of attainment – the universe remains intrinsically dualistic: we are, after all, dealing with an experiencer and that which is experienced.

It is also worth emphasizing that the word *ecstasy* (from the Greek *ex* meaning 'out' and *histanai* 'to cause to stand') means to stand outside oneself, so the very concept of ecstasy has a dualistic foundation. The Neoplatonic philosopher Plotinus wrote in his *Fourth Ennead*: 'Many times it has happened: lifted out of the body into myself; becoming external to all other things and self-encentred; beholding marvellous beauty.' As David Black has commented in his book on out-of-the-body consciousness.

> This ecstasy...was in Plotinus's philosophy only a way station on the route to transcendental union with the All. First consciousness separates from the physical and fixes itself in a particular point in space and time; and then consciousness releases the ego, like a rocket dropping its second stage as it roars out of earth orbit, and returns egoless to God.[10]

The current research into OBE and NDE consciousness is a twentieth-century counterpart to the third century Neoplatonism of Plotinus. Here we have a re-emergence of the essentially Gnostic concept that the visionary journey begins when consciousness transcends the restrictions of bodily awareness. As we see both in the paranormal literature describing OBE/NDE awareness and also in the case of the spontaneous illumination of J. Trevor in the hills beyond Macclesfield, a basic shift of consciousness has to occur. The restrictive filters which inhibit physical perception are diminished or removed and a new domain of ec-static awareness is gradually revealed in their place. It is precisely for this reason that meditators close their eyes, mystics retreat to the dark solitude of a cave and neurophysiologists like Dr John Lilly explore altered states of consciousness in flotation tanks. Similarly, the shaman journeys in the spirit vision by 'breaking through in plane' from the physical world to the mystical and magical domains beyond familiar reality. It is only in psychospiritual space that the miracle of self-transformation occurs: dualism is intrinsic to the visionary process. The key task for all visionaries is to bring back into human awareness the rich insights of inner exploration: to amalgamate these revelations within one's daily life.

Let us consider now the different categories within the OBE/NDE experience. As we have seen, many experiences of this sort involve a substantially 'physical' frame of reference. Many subjects perceive themselves to be just slightly dissociated from the physical plane of events - perhaps observing their sleeping bodies, venturing into the sky above the house or observing themselves being resuscitated by a doctor in a hospital. In such instances it is not uncommon for subjects also to hear and accurately report specific conversations which have taken place at the time.

At a more removed level - perhaps a level that brings the subject closer to physical death - a different experiential domain reveals itself: one that D. Scott Rogo has called 'eschatological'. It is here that the OBE/NDE subject may have visionary, religious or spiritual experiences - usually shaped by cultural expectations or by the person's individual belief system. Sometimes there seems to be a continuum between the physical and visionary planes, as reported by Allan Lewis and also by OBE explorer Robert Monroe (see Appendix 1). The visionary material itself can be of varying degrees of profundity: it may be somewhat dreamlike - a surreal flow of images essentially linked to one's own 'biographical' frame of reference (to use a term of Dr Stanislav Grof's), or it may contain powerful and profound archetypal sequences. In the latter realms OBE/NDE subjects may report encounters with celestial beings, superhuman beings from classical mythology, or 'God'. And sometimes they even transcend these levels of imagery, experiencing a dissolving of personal boundaries as the ego melts into other beings or seems to unite with the entire manifested universe.

As researcher Dr Kenneth Ring has recently indicated, however, the almost universal occurrence of 'positive' altered states during the NDE may simply be a mapping of one's initial contact with the Inner Light and may by no means represent the total spectrum of the visionary terrain. If *The Tibetan Book of the Dead* is correct, at the point of physical death – the ultimate act of dissociation – we will all encounter the Great Light and the positive deities (or archetypes) of the psyche first, and the negative images later. If we are unable to transcend these powerful visionary encounters on the post-mortem planes of consciousness we may then find ourselves gradually drawn back to more tangible dimensions of awareness prior to being reborn into a new incarnation.

It is highly significant that in Ring's *Life at Death* survey, over 90 per cent of 'core' NDE experience felt that their bodies and also time and space were 'no longer meaningful constructs'. In the essentially 'fluid' dimension accessed in the more transcendental NDEs one apparently enters a realm of consciousness where conceptual limitations are the only boundaries. Here visionary material from the more diffuse realms of the psyche may coexist alongside more physically based perceptions and imagery (meetings with deceased relatives in celestial environments, encounters with 'God' seated on a throne etc.) As mentioned earlier, though, even in these apparently ethereal dissociative states, the NDE/OBE experiencer still feels 'coherent' and is likely to retain an imaginal form or body shape. This body shape is evidently no more restrictive than thought itself, since its movements and actions are guided by will-power alone. When such dissociated body forms or 'thought forms' are seen by others – usually themselves in some sort of altered state like reverie, near-sleep or sensory isolation – these forms are literally 'apparitions of the living' or 'astral projections'. If such forms are those of deceased beings – those who have passed through the final, as distinct from the near-death experience (FDE) – they are perceived as ghosts and phantoms. If, perhaps, a strongly emotional event accompanied the death of that person, the apparition might then become psychically linked to that locale: hauntings thus seem best explained as discarnate energy forms (with or without consciousness – refer to the Crookall hypothesis mentioned earlier) associated with specific personal events and physical locations. However, if my own dissociative experiences with ketamine hydrochloride are any indication (and several parapsychologists have drawn a parallel between ketamine anaesthesia and the near-death experience), there may also be times in the OBE state when it is difficult to focus on a specifically physical level of existence because the range of available sensory data is so much greater. During ketamine-induced dissociation, many different planes of reality seem to coexist and to have equal validity within the spectrum of consciousness. So, confirming a point that Robert Monroe has also made, discarnate beings might find it hard to communicate with the living after death for precisely the same reason: it would be like existing on a different frequency of the 'consciousness wave-band' and trying to communicate with beings attuned by the very nature of their psycho-physical 'density' to another channel.

Despite my reluctance to formulate frameworks of consciousness because of their inherent limitations, I feel obliged to offer a model of states of consciousness accessed in the OBE/NDE states (Tables 1 and 2). All of the levels shown here, of course, would also pertain in the FDE (physical death) state.

Although Ken Wilber and Daniel Goleman might disagree, I equate the total dissolution of the ego with physical death. It seems to me to be inherently contradictory that any mystic could claim total and absolute dissolution within the Void and subsequently return to waking consciousness. In my view, the mystical experience we call 'cosmic consciousness' is but a brief glimpse across the 'borderline' of what Daniel Goleman calls 'pseudo-Nirvana' into the formlessness of the Infinite Void that lies beyond. For such a peak experience to be sustained (it never is, in fact) would necessarily involve the dissolution of one's very limited, inherently finite, physical form.

Table 1 presents the 'positive' aspects of the terrain accessed

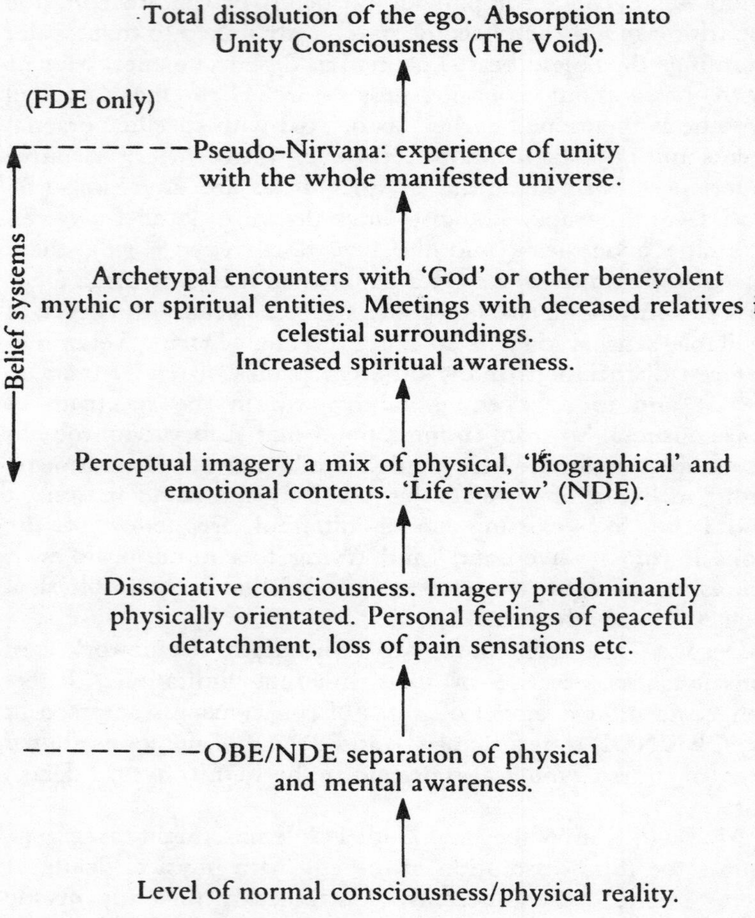

Table 1: Positive Polarities of Dissociative Consciousness
(Note: this is characterized by increasing spiritual awareness and varying levels of mystical transcendence)

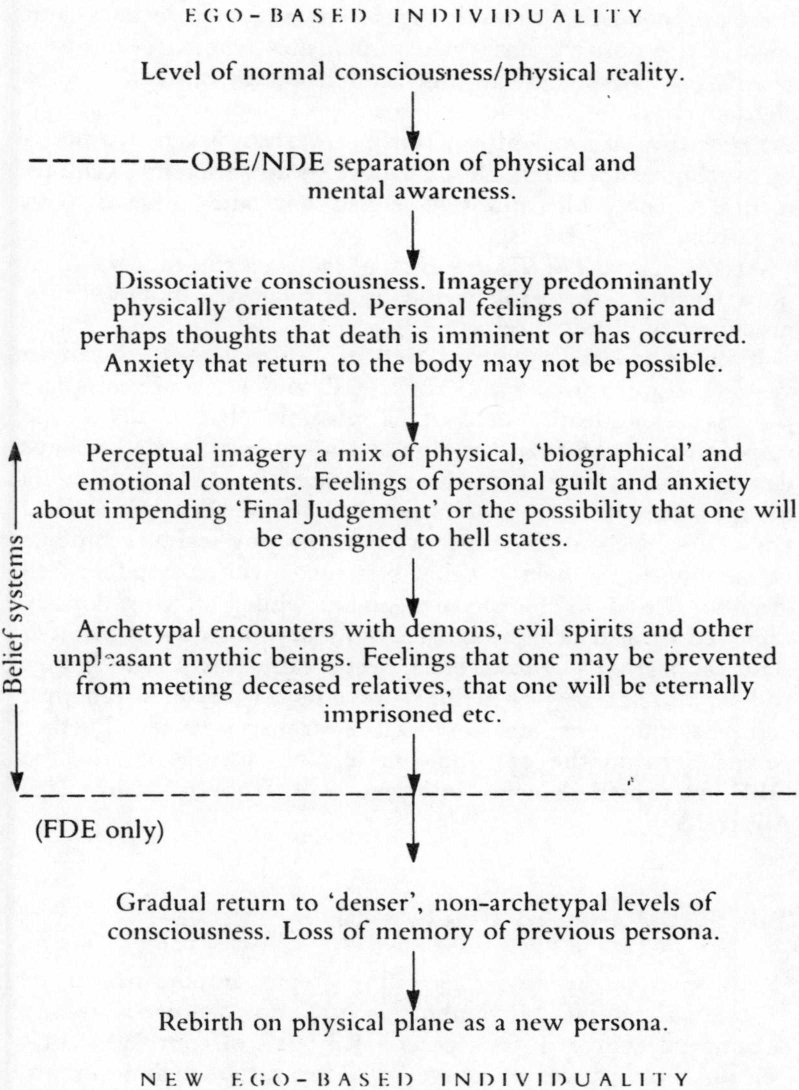

EGO-BASED INDIVIDUALITY

Level of normal consciousness/physical reality.

↓

--------OBE/NDE separation of physical and mental awareness.

↓

Dissociative consciousness. Imagery predominantly physically orientated. Personal feelings of panic and perhaps thoughts that death is imminent or has occurred. Anxiety that return to the body may not be possible.

↓

Perceptual imagery a mix of physical, 'biographical' and emotional contents. Feelings of personal guilt and anxiety about impending 'Final Judgement' or the possibility that one will be consigned to hell states.

↓

Archetypal encounters with demons, evil spirits and other unpleasant mythic beings. Feelings that one may be prevented from meeting deceased relatives, that one will be eternally imprisoned etc.

(Belief systems — spanning the three preceding stages)

↓

(FDE only)

↓

Gradual return to 'denser', non-archetypal levels of consciousness. Loss of memory of previous persona.

↓

Rebirth on physical plane as a new persona.

NEW EGO-BASED INDIVIDUALITY

Table 2: Negative Polarities of Dissociative Consciousness
(Note: this is characterized by the continuing attachment to the wheel of rebirth, according to Eastern mystical traditions)

through the OBE/NDE. However, as John Lilly has indicated, there are 'polarities' to all transpersonal levels of awareness and each of the positive states of consciousness shown here has a possible negative correlate that should not be ignored. I have characterized the latter as a 'descent' in consciousness since on the spectrum of awareness within the western psyche (as noted by psychotherapists like Desoille and Caslant) we tend to equate mental ascent with positive experience and descent with negativity (see Table 2).

According to *The Tibetan Book of the Dead* the descent from pure spirit to the grosser planes of material imagery is a precursor of physical rebirth.

If processes like those outlined in Tables 1 and 2 occur in varying degrees during the OBE/NDE, and as a more complete process after death, then it is possible that a discarnate consciousness can reside on any of a number of levels, perhaps determined by the vibrational frequency of that person's thought content, or psychospiritual being. Some deceased persons – for example, those with strong physical attachments or comparatively barren belief systems – will perhaps tend to gravitate closer to the physical plane, while still vibrationally removed from it because of their now permanently dissociated state (apparitions, ghosts etc.), while other discarnate beings will absorb themselves within the imagery of their religious belief systems or move towards transcendence. Further perspectives on the post-mortem terrain accessed during the OBE are provided in my interview with Robert Monroe (see Appendix 1).

The Relevance of Shamanism

While shamanism is now assuming greater importance in the Human Potential Movement, it has not featured to any substantial degree in transpersonal models of consciousness – perhaps because of its image as a 'primitive' belief system. However, such categorization would seem to miss the point altogether. Dating back some 15,000 years, shamanism is historically the earliest of all visionary techniques for entering altered states of consciousness and has been a characteristic of hunter-gatherer societies in many different cultures. However, as anthropologist Dr Michael Harner has shown, it is also possible to distil from the different cultural variants a core shamanic method for entering altered states of consciousness. This method, which uses a mantric drum-beat as an energy source and employs the meditative visualization that one is journeying through a tunnel into other dimensions of mystical reality, is not only experientially effective but has been compared by many to the NDE. In traditional societies shamans are often known as 'masters of death' and they have been defined by Mircea Eliade as ecstatics capable of making a visionary journey from one plane of reality to another. This journey is nothing other than a psychospiritual venture into altered states of consciousness, and traditionally involved meetings between the shaman and cosmic beings regarded as the 'gods' or 'ancestors' of the culture. In a contemporary setting, however, it is possible to adapt the technique as a means of exploring the western psyche – both for self-knowledge and healing purposes.

Readers interested in exploring this subject further may like to consult Dr Harner's *The Way of the Shaman* or my own *Elements of Shamanism*, but the point I would like to make here is that, at core, the shamanic methodology provides access to states of consciousness remarkably similar to those encountered during the NDE/OBE. Basically, the shamanic approach is characterized by a dissociative trance journey where full consciousness is retained at all times by the person venturing into the altered state. As the shaman travels in his 'mind's eye' an experiential shift is made towards inner planes of awareness and the shaman is able to explore the 'dreamtime' of the psyche by interacting with the visionary and symbolic images that rise up into consciousness. Here, as with the OBE/NDE, the shaman may encounter archetypal gods and goddesses and mythical beings, experience the OBE sensation of flying and also participate in symbolic processes of initiatory death, self-transformation and psychospiritual rebirth.

The shamanic model of the universe is extremely simple but resembles the OBE/NDE model described in Tables 1 and 2. As shown in Table 3, the vertical axis in the shaman's universe is symbolized by the Tree of Life (the World Tree) through which the shaman passes, via the branches and roots, to the magical/mystical world beyond. Here, through encounters with

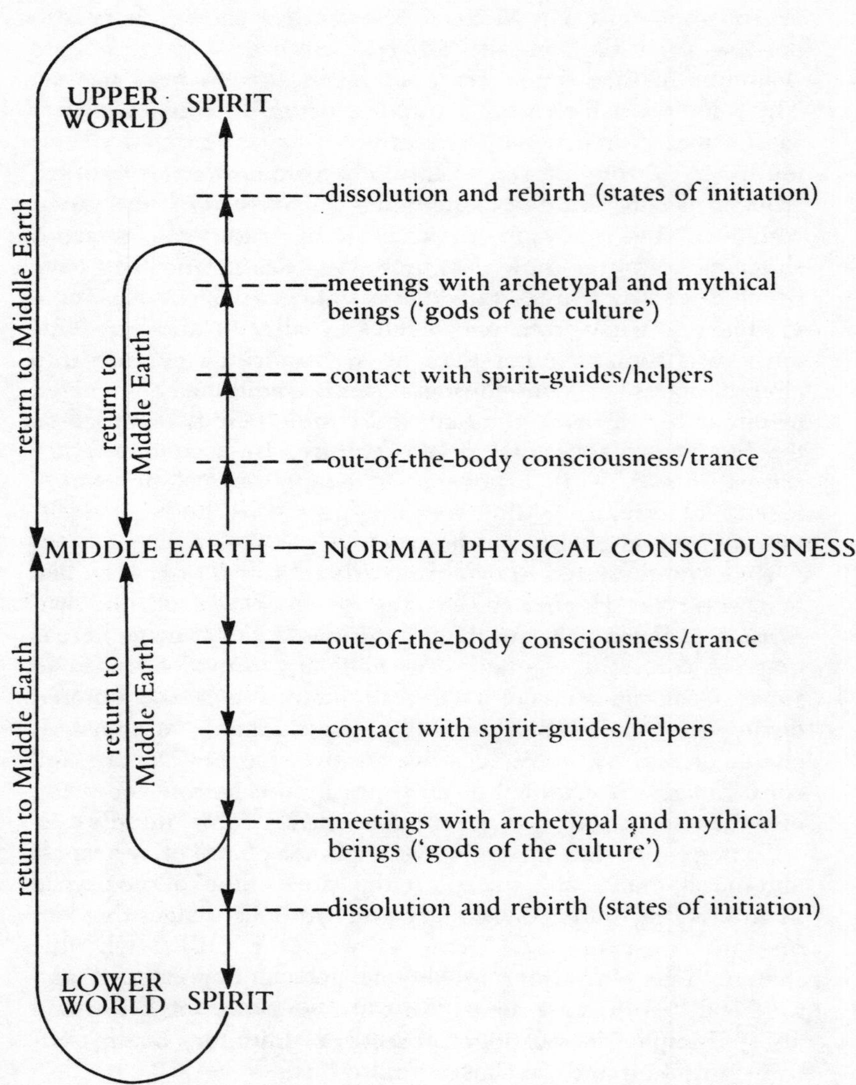

Table 3: The Shaman's Universe

(Note: this is characterized by ascent and descent on the World Tree and the breakthrough in trance consciousness from one plane to another)

spirit-helpers, the shaman is able to explore the visionary terrain beyond normal physical consciousness.

While shamans often refer to an 'upper' and a 'lower' world, these domains often tend to merge into one, and the polarity of 'good' and 'evil' associated with 'ascent' and 'descent' in the western psyche seems not to apply. It is of course possible to have terrifying as well as integrative and transcendental visionary experiences during the shamanic journey, but one needs to recognize these images as potent symbols associated with the strengthening of one's personal resolve in the quest for spiritual wisdom and healing. The shaman returns to earth-consciousness with the same sorts of 'spiritual revelations' as those gained in transcendental NDE's and in traditional shamanic societies such revelations become part of that culture's accumulated 'wisdom teaching'.

It is worth recalling the shamanic concept referred to earlier in this book, that the universe is alive with gods and spirits and that, as the Jivaro Indians of Ecuador maintain, the greatest insights into truth and causality may be gained by entering the 'supernatural' world. In modern western society we may no longer regard the world of the paranormal as 'supernatural' – indeed, the NDE and OBE are increasingly commonplace and simply represent a fascinating dimension of normal human experience. However, the principle is clear enough. It seems to me that the shamans of pre-literate hunter-gatherer societies have been attuned to the universe in ways we are only now beginning to understand.

The Visionary Human

What, then, are the implications which flow from our exploration of mystical consciousness and paranormal states? The first point one can make is that what we take to be our normal state of consciousness – our day-to-day reality – is clearly only part of a much broader spectrum of awareness. When we explore the wider terrain of inner space we open ourselves to the images and archetypes from the sacred areas of the mind that have inspired mythologies, religions and artistic endeavour in all parts of the world. At that time, too, we become increasingly familiar with the polarities of consciousness: those positive and negative, good and evil, integrative and destructive tendencies which all explorers of the psychic depths acknowledge. Yet it is only by acknowledging and amalgamating these forces within our being, and then transcending them, that we can be truly liberated.

Access to the sacred images of the psyche invariably evokes a sense of awe – one subsequently feels privileged to have encountered such profound and transformative energies. This is why prophets and shamans sometimes embody a type of divine madness – they have glimpsed the Greater Mystery, they have been seized by its sacred power, and they have then sought to communicate that feeling to others.

The transpersonal movement, and on a more general level the New Age, call us, however, in a way that I think has enduring implications for religious belief and doctrinal orthodoxy. The message now is that we should all seek to be visionaries ourselves, to explore every way possible to expand our perceptual horizons and conjure the images and revelations from the wellsprings of the psyche. Each of us will find that sacred source in different ways. It may be that some of us will embrace the infinite through some form of guru or spiritual teacher. Some will reach the spiritual realms through meditation, shamanic journeying or devotional prayer, and others by wandering in wilderness regions, mountains or rainforests and opening themselves to the rhythms and harmonies of Nature.

I don't think that it is important any more to insist on the essential 'rightness' of any specific religious path, for what will open one person to the sacred and infinite might seem inappropriate to another. The question will surely be for each of us: is the path that I am following broad enough to embrace all the possibilities of mind and spirit that clearly exist? Are the practices and teachings I am pursuing essentially liberating or restrictive? Do they encourage the possibilities for inner personal growth and connectedness with others – thus leading eventually to profound possibilities for social transformation – or do they perpetuate an outdated and restrictive belief system? In the end, each of us will have to decide this for ourselves.

It seems to me, though, that we stand at a very interesting crossroads in spiritual history. We can either embrace the evidence of consciousness research that now abounds all around us, and use it to build new paradigms for human development, or we can retreat into the security of the formal doctrinal belief systems which have persisted for centuries as explanations of the perceived relationship between humanity and 'God'. All about us are signs that some sections of society are opting for the easier doctrinal course.

It is all too easy, as the fundamentalist Muslims have done, to brand a writer like Salman Rushdie an infidel and blasphemer for offending Allah and the memory of Muhammad. Such an approach soon appears trivial and misguided if we examine it closely. Muhammad was simply a human being who was privileged to have a visionary encounter with Gabriel on Mount Hira, and Allah – if the models of consciousness we have been exploring are in any sense correct – is but one of many appellations for a transcendent reality which extends far beyond any petty human offence the fundamentalists might seize on.

In March 1990 it was announced that a legal action was underway in the British High Court to extend the laws of blasphemy beyond Christianity to other religions as well – so that Rushdie could be formally prosecuted for publishing his book *The Satanic Verses*. However the very notion of blasphemy itself – the idea that God could somehow be offended or embarrassed by human actions – is hopelessly outmoded and reflects an extremely limited awareness of what transcendental spiritual reality is all about. Here we have an essentially tribal notion of God, the concept of a spiritual overlord or ruler who, through the medium of a chosen prophet, has provided mankind with a revelation that must be obeyed at all costs. The evidence of transpersonal research, however, suggests that such a concept is nothing short of farcical. For any prophet or visionary to claim exclusive access to transcendent realms of awareness is manifestly misleading, for clearly these mystical realities are potentially available to all of us – if we can remove the restrictive filters which confine our spectrum of awareness. We should therefore do all we can to ensure that our belief systems are reinforced by personal experience of the deep inner realities. At the same time we may also need to remind ourselves that the path we have chosen is but one of many possibilities – an essential attitude, it seems to me, if we are to have any hope of engendering religious tolerance and feelings of personal humility.

Throughout human history the revelations and teachings of

religious visionaries have been filtered and interpreted by people in positions of authority and political influence who have not adequately explored the sacred realms themselves. While mystical experience brings with it an intrinsic feeling of liberation and certainty – the 'This is IT' of Alan Watts – the insistence on formal belief and dogma in the established religious institutions has a completely constricting effect on the consciousness of the devotee or follower. By way of contrast, by adopting the transpersonal approach, we can map our belief systems on the spectrum of altered states of consciousness, we can evaluate the range of perceptual possibilities accessed through different spiritual teachings, and we can make our religions 'accountable' as metaphors of transcendent realities. As I mentioned earlier, a new pragmatism is in the air. We can now ask while we are engaged in our exploration of mystical techniques and approaches: will this work, will it take me in the direction I wish to go?

The paranormal evidence referred to in the previous chapter seems to me to be very exciting indeed, for it opens us to the possibility of parallel universes. We have so long assumed, as the material reductionists would have us believe, that our thoughts and inspirations – even our consciousness itself – are simply by-products of the physical brain. However the OBE and NDE evidence points increasingly to consciousness itself as the determinant of experiential reality. In their visionary explorations, mystics see without the use of physical eyes and enter realms of awareness far beyond the confines of physical sensory input. As the Gnostics correctly surmised, we have to learn to awaken into consciousness from the dark caverns of our limited perception.

At this time in cultural history and perhaps for the first time on a wide scale in society, our belief systems and paradigms can be formulated on the basis of what we have *experienced* rather than what we have hoped for or been brought up to believe. In this way, shared inner knowledge – or *gnosis* – rather than faith in things as yet unknown will be the crucial determinant for spiritual authenticity. In the past visionaries have often been 'outsiders' in society – they have frequently lived reclusive lives or, especially in the field of artistic creativity, they have been shunned as insane or unbalanced non-conformists. This has often arisen because the 'realities' glimpsed in the visionary process have appeared as a threat or a challenge to mainstream values and perceptions. It seems to me, however, that there is now scope for the visionary to assume a more mainstream role in society.

We may well be entering a new phase in history which will see the gradual diminution of formal religious structures and their replacement not by empty nihilism or reductionist materialism but by frameworks of belief based on experiential consciousness research. As our notions of spiritual liberation, of heaven and hell and 'saviours', and the whole process of revelation itself, are modified by what we can discover through meditation, shamanic journeying or OBE exploration (to name just a few pathways to inner space), we will surely arrive at a position where we will no longer hold to a doctrinal viewpoint because we *believe* it to be so, but because it is part of a paradigm which has evolved through systematic research into states of consciousness. Without such an approach it would be difficult to sustain the notion that our individual spiritual perspectives bear any relation to 'reality'.

So, if each of us, in varying degrees and according to our various creative capacities, can begin to approach the universe from a visionary perspective, we will discover that profound revelations lie ahead. The cosmos awaits our arrival.

Notes

Chapter One: Beyond Appearances

1. Charles Tart, 'Science, States of Consciousness and Spiritual Experience: The Need for State-Specific Sciences' in C. Tart (ed.), *Transpersonal Psychologies*, Harper & Row, New York 1975
2. R. Ornstein, *The Psychology of Consciousness*, p. 17
3. M. & N. Samuels, *Seeing with the Mind's Eye*, p. 181
4. R.L. Gregory, *Eye and Brain*, p. 141
5. S. Rose, *The Conscious Brain*, p. 269
6. Gunther S. Stent, 'Can We Explain the Mind?', *Encounter*, March 1990, p. 61
7. N. Drury, 'Computers, Consciousness and Creativity – an interview with Dr Timothy Leary', *Nature & Health* Vol. 11, No. 2, 1990
8. Arthur J. Deikman, 'Comments on the GAP (Group for the Advancement of Psychiatry) Report on Mysticism' in D. Goleman and R. Davidson (eds.), *Consciousness: Brain, States of Awareness and Mysticism*, Harper & Row, New York 1979, p. 191
9. Quoted in E. Kris & O. Kurz, *Legend, Myth and Magic in the Image of the Artist*, Yale University Press, New Haven and London 1979, pp. 127–8

Chapter Two: Mystical Origins

1. Sukumar Dutt, *The Buddha and Five After-Centuries*, Luzac & Co., London 1957, p. 39
2. Matthew 1: 20–21
3. This is a theory proposed by theologian Dr Barbara Thiering, author of *The Gospels and Qumran*, Australian and New Zealand Studies in Theology and Religion, Sydney 1981
4. Mark 1: 10–11
5. See also W. Kaufmann, *Religions in Four Dimensions*, p. 121
6. Quoted in William James, *The Varieties of Religious Experience*, pp. 396–7
7. See Allan Cott, *Fasting: The Ultimate Diet*, Bantam Books, New York, 1975, p. 121
8. See Violet MacDermot, *The Cult of the Seer in the Ancient Middle East*, University of California Press, Berkeley 1971, p. 41
9. Readers are referred to Dr Grof's books *Beyond the Brain*, 1985, and *The Adventure of Self-Discovery*, 1988, for further information on holotropic therapy

10 W.B. Yeats, *Mythologies*, Macmillan, London 1962, p. 288

Chapter Three: The Visionary Landscape

1. Robert S. de Ropp, 'Self Transcendence and Beyond' in John White (ed.), *The Highest State of Consciousness*, Anchor/Doubleday, New York 1972, p. 95
2. R.M. Bucke, *Cosmic Consciousness*, p. 8
3. Ibid., p. 67
4. Quoted in John White (ed.), *The Highest State of Consciousness*, p. 103
5. Theos Bernard, *Hatha Yoga*, Rider & Co., London 1950
6. Alan Watts, *This is It, and Other Essays on Zen and Spiritual Experience*, pp. 29–31
7. Quoted in Aldous Huxley, *The Perennial Philosophy*, p. 69
8. Marcel Brion, *Ernst Fuchs*, Abrams, New York 1979, p. 6
9. N. Drury, *Inner Visions*, p. 73
10. See Lucy Lippard (ed.) *Surrealists on Art*, Prentice-Hall, New Jersey 1970, p. 121
11. Marcel Brion, *Ernst Fuchs*, pp. 22–3
12. Ibid., p. 32
13. Ibid., p. 189
14. Jolande Jacobi, *The Psychology of C.G. Jung*, p. 47
15. E.A. Wallis Budge, *The Egyptian Heaven and Hell*, p. xii
16. See N. Drury, *Don Juan, Mescalito and Modern Magic*, p. 74
17. See also W.Y. Evans-Wentz, *The Tibetan Book of the Dead*, Oxford University Press, New York 1960

Chapter Four: Dimensions of the Paranormal

1. Quoted in Joan Halifax, *Shaman: the Wounded Healer*, p. 6
2. M. Harner, *The Jivaro*, Robert Hale, London 1972, p. 134
3. See N. Drury, 'Far Journeys: The Cosmic Travels of Robert Monroe', *Nature & Health* Vol. 8, No. 4, 1987, pp. 26–9
4. Sylvan Muldoon, *The Case for Astral Projection*, Aries Press, Chicago 1936, pp. 115–16
5. N. Drury and G. Tillett, *Other Temples, Other Gods*, Methuen, Sydney 1980, pp. 159–62
6. Quoted in Carol Zaleski, *Otherworld Journeys*, p. 29
7. Ibid., pp. 102–3
8. Kenneth Ring, *Life at Death*, pp. 96–7
9. See Michael Sabom, *Recollections of Death*
10. Susan Blackmore, 'Visions of the World Beyond', *The Australian*, 14 May 1988 (reprinted from *The New Scientist*)
11. D. Scott Rogo, *The Return from Silence*, p. 192
12. Michael Sabom, *Recollections of Death* pp 70–1
13. See D. Scott Rogo, *The Return from Silence*, p. 162
14. Quoted in Z. Hagon, *Channelling*, Prism Press, Dorset 1989, p. 97
15. B. Elder, *And When I Die, Will I Be Dead?*
16. D. Scott Rogo, *The Return from Silence*, p. 240
17. Quoted in Andrew MacKenzie, *Hauntings and Apparitions*, p. 50

18. Ibid., p. 51
19. Ibid., p. 52
20. Ibid., p. 53
21. Ibid., p. 57
22. Ibid., p. 224
23. Brian Inglis, *The Paranormal*, p. 73
24. Quoted in *Into the Unknown*, Readers Digest Books, Sydney 1982, p. 176
25. R. Bayless, *Apparitions and Survival of Death*, p. 150
26. Subsequently published in E. Bauman *et al.* (eds.) *The Holistic Health Handbook*, And/Or Press, Berkeley 1978. Revised edition, edited by S. Bliss, 1985
27. Ibid., p. 353
28. S. Grof, *The Adventure of Self-Discovery*, pp. 109–10
29. Celia Green and Charles McCreery, *Apparitions*, pp. 77–8
30. Ibid., p. 4
31. A. Ellison, *The Reality of the Paranormal*, p. 19
32. Crookall was a prolific author in the paranormal field. Readers are referred to his books *The Study and Practice of Astral Projection* and *More Astral Projections*

Chapter Five: In Search of New Paradigms

1. See Elisabeth Kubler-Ross, 'Death Does Not Exist' in E. Bauman *et al.* (eds.) *The Holistic Health Handbook* and Herbert Greenhouse, *The Astral Journey*, Avon, New York 1974, pp. 311 *et. seq.* and pp. 336–7
2. Aldous Huxley, 'Drugs That Shape Men's Minds', *Saturday Evening Post*, 18 October 1958, pp. 111–13
3. Readers interested in contacting the Albert Hofmann Foundation should write to 132 West Channel Road, Suite 324, Santa Monica, CA 90402, USA (Tel. 213–281 8110)
4. For further details on Gurdjieffian vibrational numbers see P.D. Ouspensky, *The Fourth Way* (London 1957) and *In Search of the Miraculous* (London 1950)
5. This essay is included in R.N. Walsh and F. Vaughan (eds.) *Beyond Ego: Transpersonal Dimensions in Psychology*
6. Interview with the author, Esalen Institute, Big Sur 1984
7. S. Grof, 'Modern Consciousness Research and the Quest for a New Paradigm', *Re-Vision*, Vol. 2, No. 1, Winter/Spring 1979, pp 42–3
8. Roland Fischer, 'A Cartography of the Ecstatic and Meditative States' in Richard Woods (ed.) *Understanding Mysticism*, Image Books/Doubleday, New York 1980, p. 294
9. Ibid. p. 297
10. David Black, *Ekstasy*, Bobbs-Merrill, Indianopolis 1975, p. 31

APPENDIX 1

Journeys Beyond the Body – an Interview with Robert Monroe

For a man who is one of the towering figures in the study of altered states of consciousness, Robert Monroe is an extremely down-to-earth and unassuming person.

When I met him at his vast wooded property, overlooking the Blue Ridge Mountains in Virginia, the former broadcasting executive was wearing a peaked cap and slightly dishevelled casual clothes. His smile was warm, his eyes especially bright and alert for a man in his seventies, and the stubble on his chin gave him the look of a farmer who had been out all day on his tractor and forgotten to shave. This impressed me greatly – there was no pretension here. The Human Potential Movement has its fair share of prima donnas but Robert Monroe certainly isn't among them. He is simply a man who began having OBEs in the late 1950s and, since that time, has been quietly charting the terrain of inner space.

Monroe has documented his paranormal adventures in his books *Journeys Out Of The Body* and *Far Journeys*, and his new book *The Ultimate Journey* is nearing completion. These days, under the auspices of the Monroe Institute, he is very concerned with documenting the processes of self-transformation which can occur in OBE states. In particular, he believes it is important for us all to move beyond our *beliefs* to a state of *knowing* – for it is only through personal experience of far-ranging states of consciousness that we can hope to formulate any authentic insights into our lives on this planet.

I spoke to him about the world-view which has emerged from his exploration of OBE states.

You are famous for your journeys out of the body – into realms that many would equate with death, or discarnate reality. So could we start, perhaps with your definition of life?

One of my favourite acronyms is L.I.F.E. – 'layered, intelligence-forming energy'. If you think of life in this way, then we are all an expression of that energy and it also permeates all living organisms. Some people are inclined to think only of carbon-based molecules as containing living organisms. But life is much more than that if we view it as layered, intelligence-forming energy.

How do you view the transition through death – you must have seen many people dying while you yourself are in a state of out-of-the-body consciousness?

In the out-of-the-body state it is relatively easy to find someone who is just in the process of dying. However, it takes guts to do so. There are often intense dynamics in this situation – some ex-physicals get very angry and want to express their anger while others don't believe they *are* dead, no matter how hard you try to convince them they are. But the logic may suddenly dawn when a man's hand goes through the body of the woman he is trying to fondle...You may have to show that person where to go after he has died. Some cases are that simple, while others can't be convinced.

When you are guiding people who have recently died – where exactly do you guide them?

An interesting phenomenon takes place – I use the 'helping hand' approach. I take the hand of the person who has died – they still feel very physical to me because they are still attuned to being alive. Then I go towards what I call the 'belief system' territories. The people soon find themselves moving along exit routes towards these belief systems and then, all of a sudden, they just disappear. I am no longer holding their hand – they have spotted what they believe in, and have released themselves from me. They have moved into that non-physical reality which is their belief system.

Are they then trapped within the constraints of the imagery of that belief system?

There are all sorts of things to consider. Some people believe they are going to hell because they've been bad – and sure enough, there's a hell all right – but you can sometimes convince them that they don't have to head in that direction. I say to them 'Try it and see...' If they then move towards the heaven department – if we can call it that – they may still be bewildered if they are carrying the concept that they have been bad. But they are usually allowed to remain in the outer domains of heaven, as it were.

What is the next stage – does that realm merge into something else?

The belief system territories are very broad but from my viewpoint all of them have constraints. I'm a freedom person and any belief system with a wall in it is something I cannot be a part of. When you are moving along the pathways through these belief systems there are exit ramps – there must be hundreds of thousands of them. Yet if I have participated in a belief system – either in this lifetime or in another – then that exit ramp will be pretty clear to me. One of mine was in Catholicism and it was an existence in a previous life that I'm not very proud of, but it was part of the culture in which I lived then, some four or five hundred years ago.

The interesting thing is, though, that you can enter a given belief system but if there is just one little flaw, just one single doubt, you have to leave that domain – out you go. Everything begins to crumble.

My position on this is that we *can* find answers to these issues about belief systems and their limitations that are unemotional and intellectual. You can also pass across relevant data and details of the process to another person and say 'Here, you try it.' I can say to someone 'This is a *known* to me, not a belief. It can become a known to you, too. It will only be a belief to you until you *know* it.'

Some sceptics would say that the idea of passing through many lifetimes is itself a belief system. How would you respond to that?

I think one can find this out, quite specifically. To me reincarnation is a known, a reality. But I'm not interested in my previous lives unless they bring up something which is important *now*.

But surely if people generally had a broader grasp of the life and death process they would have a much more realistic concept about their role on the planet?

Yes, and I am quite specific about that too. I'm sorry to sound so specific, but I am only dealing from my knowns. To express it within the current scientific context you can think of the universe as a hologram in which we are participating. The price of participating in the hologram is that access to all previous memory is shut off. You could not have human consciousness, for example, if you knew that the last time you participated in physical life was as an alligator. So that is shut off. All previous knowledge and information relating to the lifetimes is within the hologram. *All* of our belief systems are within the hologram. When you step out of the hologram, as an intelligent energy that is nevertheless separate and apart from it, you are no longer human, and you are no longer part of time and space. Then you can have an experience of all your lifetimes – it is like a dream of all the things that happened within the hologram.

You have indicated in other interviews that at various times in the out-of-the-body state you have received information on various momentous events in history as if the universe were a type of living memory bank. Could you talk more about that?

Anyone who has the courage and the detachment can tap that data-base – it is available. But you must be totally prepared to accept it, because it will become a reality, not just a belief system, if you track back such energy fields which have existed within the hologram.

Is it like channelling?

No, it is quite different. Think of it this way. *You* have 'I-consciousness'. It is *you* asking the questions. No other consciousness is involved. *You* experience it, *you* gather the information from the realm of mind first-hand. I am quite sure anyone can undertake that sort of exploration if they make the commitment to do so, and practise the techniques involved.

However, at a certain point one moves into a larger domain. I call it the 'I-there' experience when I go out of phase. This consciousness has capabilities far beyond the simple 'I-consciousness' – it has a history of experience, it has receptive qualities, but the blunt truth is, it doesn't care. You become a sort of surrogate in gathering information and experience, and in acquiring 'left-brain' knowledge – all on behalf of that 'I-there' or IT consciousness.

That of course has strong implications for a person who believes in a type of human creator figure, a God who judges our acts and periodically intervenes in history. The model you are suggesting is of a universe simply being. *Just a process...*

You have to get down to the basics, and my basic is that we have become human wilfully, as it were, by entering the earth-life system. This system is finely tuned and well organized. It has its rules and its patterns but our consciousness is like an alien entering into this form of being. The earth-life system has a fundamental role: it says survive, and it means survive *physically*. It doesn't care about spirituality. So what does that survival drive mean? Well, first there is survival of self. That means providing yourself with shelter, food, water and warmth – and *reproducing*. Second to that is survival of the species. If you survive, the species survives – that's also an earth-life system rule. Out of that emerges a totally competitive factor. Every tree is competing for sunlight, air, soil, nutrients and water. All of Nature is balanced in symbiosis – it has to be, for the whole thing to work.

But we, as human consciousness, don't think that way. Human consciousness likes order rather than the competitive patterns but it is also driven by physical survival modes. But in that deep commitment to being here, physically, it tends to forget the other pattern for the most part. We forget so much of this human consciousness, or distort it. This earth-life system is a predator world so we can't help but be predators in order to exist in this world. We have come to this system for a very particular purpose, to learn certain things, and this system is exquisitely, beautifully adjusted to allow us to learn those things. We learn survival at a physical level, and we learn to manipulate energy. We also learn cause and effect, authority and responsibility – all those things we learn here as humans. But I can assure you that once you graduate from this earth-life system and move into other realities – you are God. You are God in those other realities because of what you have gathered here.

Do your explorations suggest there is a moral basis to the universe?

There *is* a moral basis but, as I know it, it is entirely different from our local traffic customs here. It's incredibly impersonal. I'm not just talking about the physical universe – that's what I mean by local traffic – I'm talking about other reality energy systems. Those in turn have their own sets of morality but they are tremendously different from ours. Some things we look down on are quite common there. Let's take the ant or insect culture, for example – where there are masses of segments in consciousness. Each has a specific task to perform and yet it is an extension of the overall consciousness and a part thereof. That's very common in other energy systems, in a non-physical way. If we begin to break ourselves down, in a way each of us is also like a bunch of different ants with different departments – our liver, our mental parts and so on.

I'm interested in a criticism that has been made of your work by Dr Ronald Siegel, who has specialized in the study of hallucinations. He says that in your out-of-the-body consciousness you are travelling in mental space, not physical space. What is your response to that?

I agree that could be a strong possibility except for certain things. Item one – how could I go and 'pinch' someone 200 miles away in the out-of-the-body state when they were not anticipating my being there and yet they returned with a bruise on the side where the pinch was made?

That seems to contradict what you said earlier when you were describing how a discarnate being passed through the body of his loved one.

I took a long time to try and figure that one out. The answer is simple. The pinch wouldn't have had any effect if the person hadn't been inside his body at the time. I was pinching the energy self of the person and it reflected in the physical body.

But couldn't the discarnate person do that as well?

Yes, a discarnate person could do the same thing and I'm sure that happens from time to time – in a sort of teasing kind of way. You've got to understand that once you become acclimatized to existing non-physically, you do have a tendency towards having a little fun. It isn't nearly so serious as it's made out to be. A lot of non-physical beings I have met enjoy themselves quite a bit – and act the 'spook' now and then. They're not doing any harm.

We hear quite a lot about 'possessing spirits' at the moment – especially from fundamentalist Christians. Is there any basis for worrying about this in the out-of-the-body state?

Over the years I have known two psychologists who are especially interested in 'multiple personality'. Within that multiple personality there can be in many cases what might be classified as 'possession': a callous or uncivil or angry person that lurks within. One of our associates participates in treating multiple personality dysfunctions and holds conversations with these various personalities. Invariably he finds a 'possessive type' in there, which has all the undesirable characteristics of the person concerned. You just say 'Go away Bill, we don't need you', and he says 'Why not?' He argues a bit but then goes away and back comes the other person.

Just getting back to the issue of hallucinations for a moment: reductionist psychologists would probably say that your out-of-the-body journeys are not based on how things are but on some sort of memory trace which your mind creates into a type of alternative reality.

There was at least a full year of out-of-the-body activity before I accepted the reality of it – what caused me to do so was the accumulation of data upon data – double-blind-type occurrences where I had no way of knowing what was happening in a given situation and participated from an out-of-the-body perspective.

Could you give me an example?

Certainly. Many years ago I had a double-blind situation set up with a psychologist in Westminster County, New York – a man named Foster Bradshaw. He lived about eight miles from us. The plan was that whenever he was home I would set up a time that he did not know about and go 'visit' him. This could be any weekend because I knew he would be home then. I said I would try this one day and I called his wife to tell her. She said, 'Oh, no, I don't think you should try today because he has a cold and he's in bed.' So I said I wouldn't, but around 3.30 that afternoon I had a feeling coming on that it would be easy to get out of my body. So I got out of my body and I thought I'd go across to Brad's to comfort him. I did this all by careful time-logging and using various other protocols we had agreed on. I headed for his home and got to the outside of his house but I couldn't figure out which room was his bedroom. So I went around to the back – and here was Brad and his wife coming out of the back door of the house. I was really astounded – he was meant to be sick. What was he doing wearing a hat and coat? I did cartwheels in the air, trying to attract his attention, but this had no effect whatsoever, but I did note very carefully what he and his wife were wearing. I watched them open the garage door, get the car out and drive away. So I thought I'd follow them, and see where they were going. At this stage, I was sure it must be a hallucination because he was supposed to be in bed, sick. Later, however, I did explore the whole house and there was nobody in bed so it had to be him out in the car with his wife.

I went back to my body, made records of my recollections and then got on the phone. Sure enough, there was nobody home. Later I checked with Foster to see what had happened. He had been in bed with a cold but he had got up, got dressed and gone with his wife to the post office to get there before 4.00 pm to collect some mail. At that particular time they came out of the back door. He was wearing a grey hat and a dark coat and his wife was ahead of him as they walked – it was *exactly* the same, in exquisite detail, as I had seen it. Now, could that have been part of a hallucination? If you have fifty or sixty of those you have to believe it is real. It certainly proved it to Brad – and he was a psychologist! I don't think he believed it for the first twenty or thirty such episodes.

When you go on those sorts of explorations do you see the full range of detail or do you tend to see more where you focus your attention?

If, for example, I came into this room where we are sitting now I would have a broad view, but not particularly focused. Unless I focused my attention I would not see all the detail. Normally, I would be inclined to focus towards the individuals there. Once focusing on a person, yes, I can perceive them very well. Sometimes I perceive them too well – and get inside their minds!

Where do you position yourself – if you do at all – within the spectrum of the Human Potential Movement? You have worked in the past with Charles Tart, you have had dialogue with Elisabeth Kubler-Ross – do you see yourself in a broad sense as part of a group of people, each of whom in his or her particular way is seeking to make sense of the universe and our relationship to it?

That's a very good question – I ponder on that a great deal. I certainly don't feel part of the 'New Age' movement. When I hear people talk about love and peace and light I wonder what they mean by this. I think pure peace would bore me. We are not here to be bored, but to evolve. An evolving consciousness is one that is creating 'knowns' out of beliefs.

I have a problem thinking that the goal is 'peace'. Living here on earth produces conflicts but these in turn produce immense growth. How could one learn anything without conflict? Conflict produces something beyond the conflict itself. Sadness is one direction, ecstasy another. I wouldn't want to live forever in ecstasy because that would bore me. Similarly with love, peace and light.

Yes, certainly. But I don't think that at its most sophisticated level the Human Potential Movement is only concerned with those things. It is more preoccupied with models of consciousness, of how the universe is structured. Some of these explanations are metaphors and are based to a greater or lesser degree on personal experience.

One does not need to know every detail of this earth-life system. One should simply *live* it, *enjoy* it to its fullest. As you do that, *that* is what you are gathering – the joys and sorrows, peaks and valleys – that's why we came here. If it were nothing but light and love – you wouldn't even know love: how can you know love without something to compare it with?

On the basis of your personal experience – your own 'knowings' rather than your beliefs – do you believe that some sort of principle like the Law of Karma operates in the universe?

No. There is recycling, but returning to live another life is an individual choice. There's no 'law' that says you have to do this. You decide to do it, because you choose to. Sometimes it is because there is an addiction to being human, and that addiction holds you here until you begin to get a broader perspective on what the whole process is. Maturity to me is release of illusions. It doesn't mean that you don't enjoy the illusions, but you can learn to recognize them for what they are.

In the New Age there is a lot of discussion about whether we can choose our parents – does that happen?

I think it's not quite as easy as it sounds. Some human consciousnesses, while temporarily non-human, are so eager to get back they'll take whatever they can get! They're not proud at all, they're not waiting for the 'right parents' or the 'right opportunity'. On the other hand there are those who have made many cycles and who are 'last-timers'. They may have a thousand years to think it all over and have released all their illusions, but they want to make one more run – maybe there is a little thing that they missed on the way through. So they make one last journey before moving on, beyond the hologram. They have recognized the universe for what it is.

Last-timers are usually rather quiet types, quietly going through their lives.

There seems to be a contradiction between the concept of reincarnation and the idea that you can meet discarnate relatives in the after-death state. Meeting dead relatives is a common theme in the near-death experience, for example, and yet the question one has to ask is when would they pass into a new incarnation and therefore not be 'available'? Is some sort of time-span involved? Do families tend to cluster together as spiritual energies?

All of that is valid, strangely enough. In the near-death experience, let's say someone moves down the tunnel and meets their grandmother. We can think of that as a belief system track that's laid out and those like you and your family are all a part of that belief system. The discarnate members of your family know about death and they can see you coming.

I recall one case where discarnate members of a family knew that one of their group was dying and they had the whole belief system set up – you know, a beautiful park with benches in it, a creation, a natural-looking environment for the dying person to meet his parents and former loved ones once again. They would appear in the park, and it was like getting off a train or welcoming an airplane.

But this is still illusory. Are you saying the energy of the deceased persons isn't really there?

They're there all right. But if your belief system does not hold to the idea of recycling, unless a crack appears in your belief system you will not recycle. However, very often the perception will dawn that you *can* have another life. How it happens is very mysterious.

When you are dealing with non-physical realities still within the hologram of this earth-consciousness, you are dealing with things which are culturally hard to accept within our belief systems. Suffice it to say that there are intelligent 'near' ex-humans – 'last-timers' – who can put together a construct of your sister who 'passed on' – extracting the details from your memory-patterns of that sister – and it is so believable that you could not discern the difference between the construct and the actual person. If that is important to you, that can be set up. There are abilities that become apparent to you in the other reality that are just extraordinary. I've had this type of thing demonstrated to me several hundred times. I've been plunged into constructs that are so real that I couldn't distinguish them from physical reality. Then there is a 'click' and I come out of it. So this tells you quite a bit about what can be done with 'intelligent energy'.

Just to define a 'last-timer' – that's a person going beyond incarnation into a new realm?

That's right – a person who could leave the hologram but who has decided wilfully not to. There is a need to do something specific in one last lifetime, and they do it. But it is not to save the world or anything like that. We humans have this idea of something being for 'the betterment of humankind'. But what are we talking about? We should be talking about 'for betterment of the dream'. If you are outside the hologram, why would you want to improve the hologram? It's much more exciting *outside* the hologram. The hologram is a designed dream-experience for a specific purpose. Once you get out of it, totally, you don't ever look back.

As humans, can we know anything beyond the hologram?

Of course you can – that's the freedom which lies beyond belief systems, beyond the hologramic self. It's an exquisite freedom.

It must be very hard to convey that, because you wouldn't want to trap such perceptions in language, or metaphors.

This is why I keep using acronyms: it's so hard to describe.

And am I right in saying that beyond the hologram we are dealing with 'intelligent energy'? Is that a fair way to describe it?

Yes, you are beyond the universe at that point. 'Being' is a totally insufficient word. So is 'God'. It's a creative process though. But who or what did the creating? That's the fun part...I describe that in some detail in my new book *The Ultimate Journey*. However, I'll say this: the big barrier is fear of physical death – get past that and you have tremendous freedom. And when you get past the 'non-physical' fears – the fears relating to what is going to happen to you when you are no longer physical – then you get to know what fun is all about!

For further information on Robert Monroe's work, contact:

The Monroe Institute
Route 1
Box 175
Faber
Virginia VA 22938
USA

Tel. (804) 361 1252

APPENDIX 2

Ambient Music as an Aid to Visionary Consciousness and Inner Health

We have already considered the role of meditation and shamanism within the spectrum of visionary consciousness. A further area which many readers will find of interest is music, especially when it is combined with different types of visualization.

The following article, which first appeared in the journal *Nature & Health*, provides an introductory overview of the use of ambient and related forms of music as a therapeutic aid to holistic wellbeing. Those who are interested in more detailed descriptions relating to the use of music for visualizations and meditations based on the esoteric traditions (Kabbalah, Tarot, Astrology, The Egyptian Book of the Dead and Kundalini Yoga) may like to consult my book *Music for Inner Space* (Prism Press, 1985).

Music has many wonderful and distinctive qualities. It can intensify our feelings, summon to mind associated images and memories, transport us into a state of awe or simply charm us through the delicacy of melody. In primitive trance rituals, frantic monotonous drumming can lead mediums into a state of spirit-possession, while in Indian music drones and mantras are used to focus the mind and lead it through its many distractions to a state of inner peace and unity.

Clearly, music speaks to us in a special way - and one of the core ingredients of music is rhythm. According to musicologists Manfred Clynes and Janice Walker, rhythm is intrinsic to animal behaviour - whether we are considering such activities as flying, walking, swimming or running - and the rhythms which characterize these movements are controlled by the programmes of the central nervous system. In man, these rhythms have become linked with the imagination and can influence our moods, our attitudes, and the way we feel. Indeed, in the extreme example of trance dancing, rhythm expresses itself in movement and gesture in such a total way that there is a complete shift of consciousness - from the everyday, familiar world to the altered state of myth and magical transformation.

Inner health is also about self-transformation, but in a more composed and self-aware way. The trance medium who is possessed by a tribal god loses consciousness and is subsumed by the incoming deity. The sort of self-transformation we are advocating here, however, is a broadening of the spectrum of inner events accompanied by full sensory awareness: a resolution of states of conflict and tension to achieve a new sense of integration and wholeness.

Exactly why music affects our state of consciousness can only be hinted at. Perhaps, for example, the experience we had as infants listening to our mother's heartbeat, and our subsequent awareness of the pattern of our breathing – a crucial factor of our existence – are directly linked to our experience of rhythm. It also seems that our awareness of time is an important factor. For most people, it appears, a rate of less than eighty beats per minute is 'slow', whereas more than ninety beats per minute is 'fast', and as we all know our perception of rhythm can have an immediate influence on our moods and feelings. A more leisurely beat tends to relax and soothe, while an up-tempo beat exhilarates and excites.

However, music has several other important qualities apart from rhythm, and these affect still further the range and qualities of our perception.

Intensity and volume: These contribute power and impact. In music, intensity arises as tones are added layer upon layer – a characteristic, for example, of most types of orchestral music. Intensity is one of the ingredients of 'carrying power' – the ability music has to literally transport us into other realms of awareness.

Timbre: This is the quality of 'richness' in music. It is often linked to volume but also to the sonic structure of the composition. Rich and 'full' music tends to be more convincing and the images it summons to mind are correspondingly more 'real'.

Consonance and dissonance: Chords in music tend to be of two kinds – those which create tension (dissonance) and those which tend towards resolution or harmony (consonance). The presence of consonance and dissonance in music creates important dynamic contrasts which have a direct effect on the listener. For most people, a 'satisfying' musical composition is one which leads the listener through a range of tonal contrasts to a state of resolution.

Music and Health

From a therapeutic point of view the music that is of most use in attaining inner health tends to take the following forms:

- Music which reduces stress or induces relaxation. This music allows us to enter a state of consciousness midway on the spectrum between normal alertness and sleep

- Music which summons specific images to mind and which can in turn be used to focus upon one's inner processes
- Music for encountering repressed or unacknowledged dimensions of the self
- Music which leads the listener through a transitionary process from one mode to another
- Music which lifts one's consciousness to a transcendental or blissful state

Each of these categories of music can be valuable in the process of attaining inner health and there are several ways in which music can be combined with visualization or meditation. One of the most accessible techniques is to combine music with guided imagery.

Guided Imagery and Visualization

Guided imagery has been used extensively in psychotherapy since the pioneering work of Robert Desoille, Eugene Caslant, Carl Happich and Hanscarl Leuner. The work originated in Europe, but has had a major impact on the Human Potential Movement, especially through popular adaptations like Robert Masters' and Jean Houston's 'mind games', the Silva Mind Control method and Alexander Everett's Mind Dynamics. It is also an integral part of the contemporary approach to cancer meditation therapy advocated by Dr Carl Simonton and Dr David Bresler.

Eugene Caslant, whose work is seminal to this process, emphasized the idea that certain meditative symbols had a particular psychological effect. Symbols of ascent like a staircase or flying chariot, for example, tended to lead the meditator towards a feeling of tranquility and self-composure, while 'descending' in the imagination could produce feelings of anxiety and fear associated with the perception of darkness.

Like Caslant, Robert Desoille also believed that the idea of ascent and descent mirrored a psychological reality and that it was present even in our language. In *The Directed Daydream* he commented:

> In both instances we are dealing with a basic law of the mind; it is expressed in everyday language when we speak of 'bright ideas', 'warm feelings' and 'lofty thoughts'. And, on the other hand, we recognise 'shady deals', 'a cool reception' and 'low deeds'.

Desoille developed the idea of leading his subjects through symbolic imaginal situations which would reveal aspects of their personal psychological makeup. This involved patterns of both ascent and descent. For example Desoille might ask his subject to imagine himself at the foot of a mountain and then to start climbing. Some patients would find this an easy task and move along at a brisk pace, while others might encounter major or insuperable obstacles. Those experiencing difficulty would be subsequently assisted with the suggestion of 'helpers' of various kinds (friends, loved ones, or even supernatural beings). Other themes employed by Desoille included the following:

Purpose	Theme
Confronting one's more suppressed characteristics	For both sexes, a descent into the depths of the ocean.
Coming to terms with the parent of the opposite sex	For a man, a descent into a cave to find a witch or a sorceress
	For a woman, a descent into a cave to find a wizard or a magician
Coming to terms with the parent of one's own sex	For a man, a descent into a cave to find a wizard or a magician
	For a woman, a descent into a cave to find a witch or a sorceress

Here, Desoille employed mythic images rather than encourage imaginal encounters with the actual people at the source of the conflict. He felt his patients would be less likely to qualify their answers and replies in dialogue with such 'imaginary' beings than with the real-life counterparts they represented.

Desoille's guided imagery approach was essentially conceived to help the patient overcome personal limitations. His approach can be summarized as follows:

> The patient must learn to control the 'archetypes' within himself, to be free of them, and thereby lose his fear of them...The goal of the technique is to direct the patient toward the fulfilment of his human potentialities through the creative development of man's basic biological impulses into a higher and harmonic idea.

For Desoille the state of religious awareness aroused in this process was the highest level of mental functioning.

Carl Happich published several writings on guided imagery in Germany in the 1930s and, like Desoille, made use of specific meditative symbols to produce a positive mental effect. These included: a meadow, a chapel and a bubbling fountain (as well as a mountain, used in much the same way as described above).

Happich used the meadow image to gauge the mental health of his patients: the balanced and happy person would invariably populate the meadow with children, flowers or images of spring. The unhappy or depressed person was more likely to visualize dying vegetation or barrenness, and conjure other negative motifs to fill the landscape.

The chapel image, on the other hand, was a symbol of the sacred centre of being, while meditating on the bubbly fountain attuned the patient to the energy source of life itself.

Happich was opposed to the use of symbols like a snake or scorpion which could stimulate dangerous or negative emotions and preferred to choose motifs which he felt sure had a positive and transforming effect.

Hanscarl Leuner developed the guided imagery techniques of Carl Happich in the 1950s and similarly advocated the use of 'positive' images. He commenced his therapy sessions with the scenes of the meadow, mountain and brook which, for most people, had an unthreatening connotation. Leuner's system, which he called 'Guided Affective Imagery' included several of the symbolic situations described above, as well as some new ones:

The Stream: More far-reaching than Happich's bubbly fountain, the image of the stream was used to represent the amount of psychic energy available to the patient, and the depth and width of the stream was taken to be indicative of character, eg 'broad-minded', 'shallow'. Obstacles in the stream were symbolic of conflicts in real life.

A House: Leuner considered the house to be an appropriate symbol of the self. The patient might start by visualizing a familiar house and then extend it or explore it in an imaginary way. The more imaginary the house, the greater the insights it provided into the makeup of the psyche. The size of each imaginary room in relation to the nature of its contents was indicative of specific personal qualities.

The Ideal Personality: The patient was asked to 'hear' in his imagination the name of a person of the same sex, and then visualize that person. Leuner found that the imaginary person often represented the qualities regarded as 'ideal' by the subject.

A Swampy Pool: Leuner would ask the subject to visualize a swampy pool in the meadow and look down into the waters. Human figures or animals that appeared in the pool, or which rose out of it, were considered to be symbolic of repressed sexuality.

An Erupting Volcano: Leuner considered this symbol an ideal gauge of inner tension. The degree of violence and the amount of material erupted were highly indicative of this inner conflict.

A Lion: Leuner asked the subject to visualize a lion and then imagine it confronting someone regarded as an opponent in real life. The reaction of the lion – eating the opponent or lying passively at his or her feet – was indicative of the subject's ability to express himself effectively and interact with competitors.

An Old Picture Book: The subject was asked to imagine a house, explore its cellar and then dig a hole in its earthen floor in order to find an old book buried there. The subject was then asked to describe some of the pictures in the book. Leuner found that his patients often referred to unresolved or unexpressed issues which had arisen in earlier sessions.

Leuner also introduced the notion of the 'inner guide' to his guided imagery work. For him this persona – whether it appeared as an animal or as a wise old man – represented the positive directions of the psyche, and the subject was encouraged to communicate with it. There were also several specific strategies for relating to images:

- In a confrontation situation the subject was encouraged to watch the encounter dispassionately rather than struggle to escape.
- The subject should ideally seek reconciliation with a hostile image rather than 'wound' or 'kill' it (after all, this counter-attack could rebound on oneself.)
- 'Magic' fluids or potions could be visualized to relieve pain.

As mentioned earlier, guided imagery is now used extensively as a health therapy in the United States. As Dr Dennis Jaffe and Dr David Bresler note in a recent article on healing imagery, we need to distinguish between the somatic and autonomic nervous systems for we can access each of these in different ways:

> Verbal thoughts most directly access the somatic nervous system, so, if for example you wish to stand up, all you need to do is think 'stand up, now' and your voluntary nervous system will co-ordinate the appropriate muscular activity. On the other hand, the language of imagery directly accesses the autonomic nervous system which regulates breathing, the heartbeat, blood chemistry, digestion, tissue regeneration and repair, immune and inflammatory responses, and many other bodily functions essential to life.

As a consequence, imagery can be used for a diverse range of health functions, from simply inducing the 'relaxation response' through to visualizing the healing of ruptured blood vessels or containing – and hopefully eliminating – the spread of cancerous tumours.

On one level such visualization has to do simply with focusing on positive outcomes: optimism is always preferable to negativity. However the visualizations can also be quite specific. Dr Carl Simonton, whose work with cancer patients is well known, uses imagery techniques to counteract the notion of cancer as 'some big powerful thing' about to overrun the body. Stimulating the patient's belief in his own curative powers, the cancer visualization might involve the image of the patient as a warring knight successfully overcoming the cancer dragon within the body, or any other pictorial metaphor that might seem appropriate to the patient. The effect is for the person with cancer to engage in his own healing process. As Dr Simonton writes:

> I try to get [the patient] to produce mental descriptions of all aspects of the disease. Through these techniques the patient begins to activate his motivation to be well and to arouse emotions and problems into the consciousness.

Recommended Music for Visualization and Meditation

Because music enhances the perception of imagery it is valuable in a broad range of meditation and visualization techniques. One simply has to select sequences from existing musical recordings which relate to the specific visualization process and, where necessary, make compilation tapes. It may be music to evoke an atmosphere, to provide a musical context for a specific image or symbol, or to transport the meditator from one imaginal locale to another.

Since guided imagery leads the subject into an altered state, it is ideal to begin with a sequence of relaxation music and then to structure the session with a series of musical environments that pertain more specifically to the process in question.

Within the genre of contemporary inner space music – which specifically caters for altered states – there is an enormous range of musical colour and texture from which to choose. This type of music also has an advantage over more traditional music in that, for the most part, it is abstract rather than melodic and is recent enough not to suggest distracting image-associations.

The following recordings provide possible musical environments for some of the themes which have been described earlier:

Music for relaxation: Aeoliah and Larkin *Inner Sanctum* (Celestial Octaves)
Harold Budd and Brian Eno *The Pearl* (EG/Polygram)
Brian Eno *Discreet Music* (Side One) (Antilles)
Brian Eno *Music for Airports* (EG/Polygram)
Steven Halpern *Eventide* (Halpern Sounds)
Paul Horn *Inside the Great Pyramid* (Mushroom)
Kitaro *Silver Cloud* (Polydor)

Music for ascent: Gyorgy Ligeti 'Requiem' from the *2001* film soundtrack (MGM) Pink Floyd 'Echoes' (last section) from *Meddle* (Harvest) Klaus Schulze 'Bayreuth Return' from *Timewind* (Virgin) Tangerine Dream 'Rubycon II' (first section) from *Rubycon* (Virgin)

Music for descent: Rajneesh Foundation musicians 'Nadabrahma' (first two-thirds) from *Nataraj/Nadabrahma* (Rajneesh Foundation International) Tangerine Dream 'Rubycon I' from *Rubycon* (Virgin) Tangerine Dream 'Logos Part One' (opening sequence) from *Logos* (Virgin)

Music for the ocean: Fripp and Eno 'Wind on Water' (first half) from *Evening Star* (Island)
Klaus Schulze 'Mindphaser' (first half) from *Moondawn* (Brain/Metronome)

Music for the meadow: Brian Eno 'Unfamiliar Wind' from *On Land* (EG/Polygram) Pink Floyd 'Grandchester Meadows' (first section) from *Ummagumma* (Harvest)

Music for the chapel: Gyorgy Ligeti 'Lux Aeterna' from the *2001* film soundtrack (MGM)

Music for the bubbling brook and stream: Edgar Froese 'Aqua' and 'Upland' from *Aqua* (Virgin)

Music for exploring the imaginal house/old picture book: Harold Budd and Brian Eno 'Their Memories' from *The Pearl* (EG/Polygram)
Rajneesh Foundation musicians 'Nadabrahma' (first two-thirds) from *Nataraj/Nadabrahma* (Rajneesh Foundation International)

Music for a swampy pool: Brian Eno 'Lizard' and 'Tal Coat' from *On Land* (EG/Polygram)

Music for an erupting volcano: Ash Ra 'Sun Rain' from *New Age of Earth* (Virgin)
Manuel Gottsching 'Echo Waves' from *Inventions for Electric Guitar* (Ohr)
Laraaji 'Dance 1' and 'Dance 2' from *Day of Radiance* (EG/Polygram)

Music for confronting a lion: Philip Glass 'The Grid' from *Koyaanisquatsi* (Island)

Workshop Exercises

Basic Relaxation: This is ideal prior to visualization and meditation exercises.

Sit in a chair or lie down on the floor in a comfortable position. Breathe deeply following this pattern: breathe in to a count of four; hold for a count of four; release to a count of four; hold for a count of four (repeat).

Now gradually release the tension from all parts of your body in sequence. Imagine a soothing impulse entering your feet and working its way up through your ankles, your calves, your knees, your thighs and into your abdomen. Let go of any tensions and allow this calming wave to flow into your chest, your arms and your neck. But don't go to sleep! Focus your awareness in your head.

Appropriate music: see relaxation music listings. Several of Steven Halpern's recordings are suitable but *Eventide* is especially soothing. Brian Eno's *Music for Airports* is also an outstanding example of the ambient style.

Guided Imagery Sessions: Select imagery sequences from Desoille, Happich or Leuner's visualization therapies which you feel would be suitable meditations either for yourself or a group of friends. If in a group situation you may like to take turns as leader, guiding your fellow meditators into different symbolic locations in turn over several sessions. In order to do this you should write descriptive 'entry' material which can be read aloud to the group to establish the symbolic setting in each case. Make these descriptions as minimal as possible so that they allow the meditator's imaginations a broad scope for self-exploration.

Begin each session with the basic relaxation technique described above and ask each participant to record the 'inner journey' in a meditation diary after each session. You might like to have group discussions afterwards.

Select music from recordings available to you or, if you prefer, make your own compilation tapes. The list given above is simply a starting point.

Enjoy your inner journeys!

Additional References

M. Clynes (editor), *Music, Mind and Brain*, Plenum, New York 1982

R. Desoille, *The Directed Daydream*, Psychosynthesis Research Foundation, New York 1966

D. Jaffe and D. Bresler, 'Guided Imagery: Healing Through the Mind's Eye' in Joseph E. Shorr, *Imagery*, Plenum, New York 1980

C. Simonton, 'The Role of the Mind in Cancer Therapy' in R.J. Carlson, *Frontiers of Science and Medicine*, Regnery, Chicago 1976

A. Watson and N. Drury *Healing Music*, Prism Press, Dorset 1987

BIBLIOGRAPHY

Abdullah, S. 'Meditation: Achieving Internal Balance' in E. Goldwag (ed.), *Inner Balance*, Prentice-Hall, New Jersey, 1979

Achterberg, J. *Imagery in Healing*, Shambhala, Boulder 1985

Bayless, R. *Apparitions and Survival of Death*, University Books, New York, 1973

—— *The Other Side of Death*, University Books, New York, 1971

Black, D. *Ekstasy*, Bobbs-Merrill, Indianapolis, 1975

Blackmore, S. *Beyond the Body*, Paladin, London, 1983

Bliss, S. (ed.) *The New Holistic Health Workbook*, Viking-Penguin, New York, 1985

Brandon, S.G.F. *The Judgment of the Dead*, Weidenfeld & Nicolson, London, 1967

Bucke, R.M. *Cosmic Consciousness*, Dutton, New York, 1901

Budge, E.A.W. *The Egyptian Heaven and Hell*, Martin Hopkinson, London, 1925

Comstock, W.R. (ed.) *Religion and Man*, Harper & Row, New York, 1971

Crookall, R. *The Study and Practice of Astral Projection*, Aquarian Press, London, 1960

——*More Astral Projections*, Aquarian Press, London, 1964

——*The Jung-Jaffe View of Out-of-the-Body Experiences*, World Fellowship Press, London, 1970

Dilman, I. *Freud and the Mind*, Basil Blackwell, Oxford, 1986

Drury, N. *Inner Visions: Explorations in Magical Consciousness*, Routledge & Kegan Paul, London, 1979

——*Don Juan, Mescalito and Modern Magic*, Arkana, London, 1985

——*Music for Inner Space*, Prism Press, Dorset, 1985

—— *The Elements of Shamanism*, Element Books, Dorset, 1989

—— *The Elements of Human Potential*, Element Books, Dorset, 1989

——(ed.) *Inner Health*, Prism Press, Dorset, 1985

Edinger, E. *Ego and Archetype*, Penguin Books, New York, 1973

Elder, B. *And When I Die, Will I Be Dead?* Australian Broadcasting Corporation, Sydney, 1987

Ellison, A. *The Reality of the Paranormal*, Harrap, London, 1988

Evans-Wentz, W.Y. (ed.) *The Tibetan Book of the Dead*, Oxford University

Press, New York, 1960

Fischer, R. 'A Cartography of the Ecstatic and Meditative States' in R. Woods, *Understanding Mysticism,* Image Books/Doubleday, New York 1980

Gettings, F. *The Occult in Art*, Rizzoli, New York, 1979

Goleman, D. *The Meditative Mind*, Tarcher, Los Angeles, 1988

Goleman, D. & Davidson, R. (eds.) *Consciousness: Brain, States of Awareness and Mysticism*, Harper & Row, New York, 1979

Green, C. & McCreery, C. *Apparitions*, Institute of Psychophysical Research, Oxford, 1989

Gregory, R.L. *Eye and Brain*, 4th Edition, Princeton University Press, New Jersey, 1990

Grey, M. *Return from Death: An Exploration of the Near-Death Experience*, Arkana, London, 1985

Grof, S. *Realms of the Human Unconscious*, Dutton, New York, 1976

——*Beyond the Brain*, State University Press of New York, Albany, 1985

——*The Adventure of Self-Discovery*, State University Press of New York, Albany, 1988

Halifax, J. *Shaman: the Wounded Healer*, Crossroad, New York, 1982

Hampden-Turner, C. *Maps of the Mind*, Mitchell Beazley, London, 1981

Harner, M. *The Jivaro*, Robert Hale, London, 1972

——*The Way of the Shaman*, Harper & Row, San Francisco, 1980

Houston, J. *The Possible Human*, Tarcher, Los Angeles, 1986

Huxley, A. *The Perennial Philosophy*, Chatto & Windus, London 1946

——*The Doors of Perception/Heaven and Hell*, Penguin Books, London, 1963

——*Moksha: Writings on Psychedelics and the Visionary Experience*, Stonehill, New York, 1977

Inglis, B. *The Paranormal*, Granada, London, 1985

Jacobi, J. *The Psychology of C.G. Jung*, Routledge & Kegan Paul, London, 1968

James, W. *The Varieties of Religious Experience*, Longman, Green & Co., London and New York, 1904

Jung, C.G. *Analytical Psychology*, Vintage Books, New York, 1968

——*Memories, Dreams, Reflections*, Random House, New York, 1961

Kaufmann, W. *Religions in Four Dimensions*, Readers Digest Press, New York 1976

Leary, T. *The Politics of Ecstasy*, Paladin, London, 1970

Lee, P.R. (ed). *Symposium on Consciousness*, Penguin, New York, 1971

Lilly, J. *The Centre of the Cyclone*, Calder and Boyars, London, 1973

——*The Human Biocomputer*, Abacus, London, 1974

——*Simulations of God*, Simon & Schuster, New York, 1976

Lings, M. *Muhammad: His Life Based on Earliest Sources*, Allen & Unwin, London, 1983

MacKenzie, A. *Hauntings and Apparitions*, Paladin, London, 1983

May, R. *Physicians of the Soul*, Amity House, New York, 1988

McGlashan, A. *Savage and Beautiful Country: The Secret Life of the Mind*, Stonehill, New York, 1967

Metzner, R. *The Ecstatic Adventure*, Macmillan, New York, 1968

——*Opening to Inner Light*, Century, London, 1987

Mitchell, J.L. *Out-of-Body Experiences*, Turnstone, Wellingborough, 1985
Monroe, R. *Journeys Out of the Body*, Doubleday, New York, 1971
——*Far Journeys*, Souvenir Press, London, 1985
Moody, R. *Life After Life*, Bantam Books, New York, 1976
——*Reflections on Life After Life*, Bantam Books, New York 1978
Nigosian, S. *Islam: The Way of Submission*, Crucible, Wellingborough, 1987
Ornstein, R. *The Psychology of Consciousness*, Cape, London, 1975
——*Multimind*, Macmillan, London, 1986
Ring, K. *Life at Death: A Scientific Investigation of the Near-Death Experience*, Coward McCann & Geoghegan, New York, 1980
——*Heading Toward Omega: In Search of the Meaning of the Near-Death Experience*, Morrow, New York, 1984
Rogo, D. Scott *Mind Beyond the Body*, Penguin Books, New York, 1978
——*Leaving the Body: A Complete Guide to Astral Projection*, Prentice-Hall, New York, 1983
——*The Return From Silence: A Study of Near-Death Experiences*, Aquarian Press, Wellingborough, 1989
Rose, S. *The Conscious Brain*, Weidenfeld & Nicolson, London, 1973
Sabom, M. *Recollections of Death*, Corgi Books, London, 1982
Saddhatissa, H. *The Buddha's Way*, Allen & Unwin, London, 1971
Samuels, M. and N. *Seeing with the Mind's Eye*, Random House/Bookworks, New York, 1975
Tart, C. (ed.) *Transpersonal Psychologies*, Harper & Row, New York, 1975
——*Altered States of Consciousness*, Wiley, New York, 1969
Valle, R.S. & von Eckartsberg, R. (ed.) *The Metaphors of Consciousness*, Plenum, New York, 1981
Walsh, R.N. & Vaughan, F. (ed.) *Beyond Ego*, Tarcher, Los Angeles, 1980
Watts, A. *The Joyous Cosmology*, Vintage Books, New York, 1962
——*This is It, and Other Essays on Zen and Spiritual Experience*, Pantheon, New York, 1960
Wilber, K. *The Spectrum of Consciousness*, Quest Books, Illinois, 1977
——*No Boundary*, Centre Publications, Los Angeles, 1979
——*Up From Eden*, Doubleday, New York, 1981
White, J. (ed.) *The Highest State of Consciousness*, Anchor Press/Doubleday, New York, 1972
Woods, R. (ed.) *Understanding Mysticism*, Image Books/Doubleday, New York, 1980
Zaleski, C. *Otherworld Journeys*, Oxford University Press, New York, 1987

Index